BEST OF Jason Mraz

Cover photo © Eric Morgensen

ISBN 978-1-5400-4290-3

Visit Hal Leonard Online at
www.halleonard.com

Contact us:
Hal Leonard
7777 West Bluemound Road
Milwaukee, WI 53213
Email: info@halleonard.com

In Europe, contact:
Hal Leonard Europe Limited
42 Wigmore Street
Marylebone, London, W1U 2RN
Email: info@halleonardeurope.com

In Australia, contact:
Hal Leonard Australia Pty. Ltd.
4 Lentara Court
Cheltenham, Victoria, 3192 Australia
Email: info@halleonard.com.au

A BEAUTIFUL MESS

Words and Music by JASON MRAZ,
MONA TAVAKOLI, CHASKA POTTER,
MAI BLOOMFIELD and BECKY GEBHARDT

You got the

best of both worlds; __ you're the kind of girl who can take down a man __ and

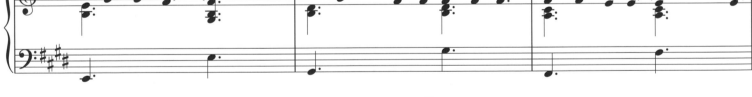

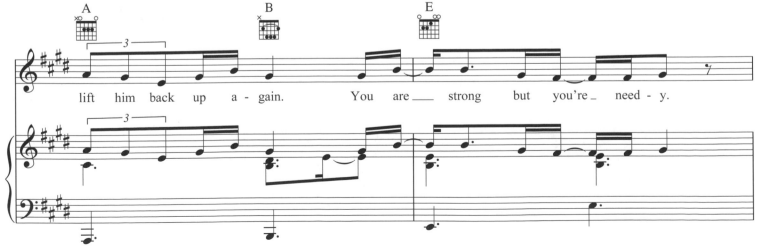

lift him back up a- gain. You are __ strong but you're __ need - y.

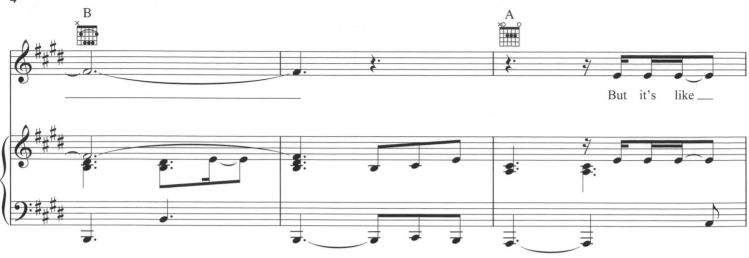

But it's like ___

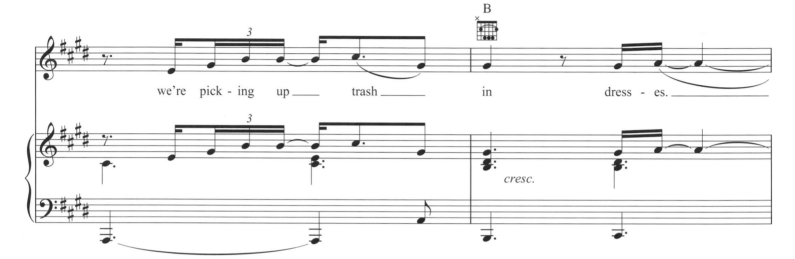

we're pick - ing up ___ trash ___ in dress - es. ___

cresc.

Well, it kind of hurts ___ when ___ the

mf

G#m7

{ kind of words ___ you write kind of turn ___ them -
{ kind of words ___ you say kind of turn ___ them -

F#m7

selves in-to knives.___ And don't / mind___ my___ nerve.___ You could
selves in-to blades.___ / Kind___ and___ cour-te-ous is a

call___ it___ fic-tion, but I / like be-ing sub-merged___ in your
life___ I've___ heard, but it's / nice to say___ that we

To Coda ⊕

con-tra-dic-tions,___ dear.___ } 'Cause here_____ we are,___
played in the dirt,___ oh,___ dear.___ }

here we are.

mp

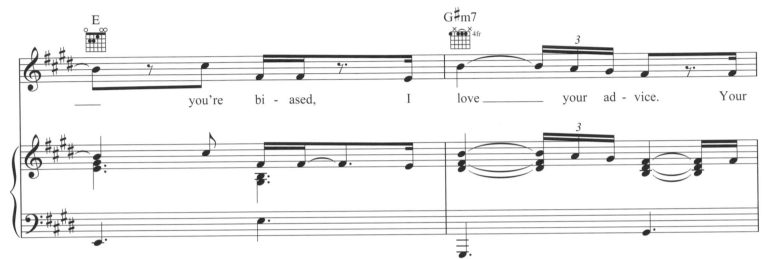

heart ___ dis - fig - ure, but that's no con - cern ___ when we're

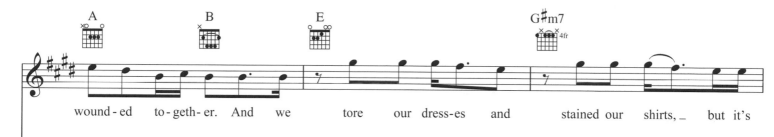

wound - ed to - geth - er. And we tore our dress - es and stained our shirts, _ but it's

Freely

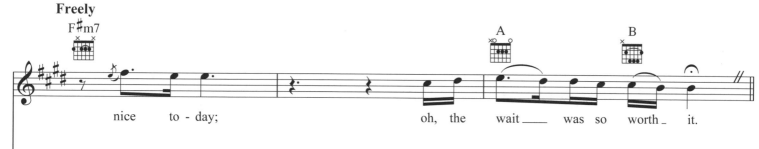

nice to - day; oh, the wait ___ was so worth _ it.

Tempo I

BEST FRIEND

Words and Music by JASON MRAZ,
BECKY GEBHARDT, CHASKA POTTER,
MAI BLOOMFIELD and MONA TAVAKOLI

Moderately slow groove

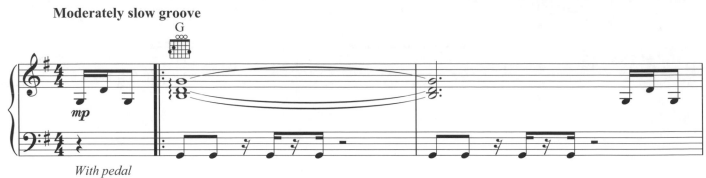

With pedal

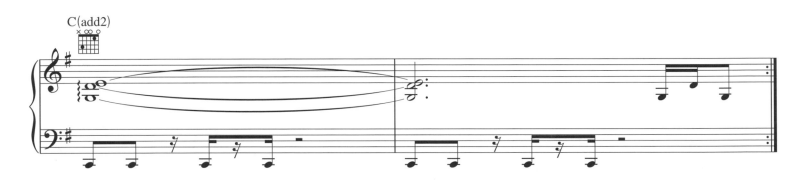

Love is where this be - gins; ____
Thank you for all of your trust. ____

thank you for let - ting me __ in. ____
Thank you for not giv - ing __ up. ____

I nev - er had to pre - tend; _____
Thank you for hold - ing my hand. _____

you've al - ways known who I _____ am. _____ And I know _____
I've al - ways known where you _____ stand. _____ Yes, I feel _____

_____ my life _____ is bet - ter _____ be-cause you're _____ a part _____ of it. I know _____

_____ with - out _____ you by _____ my side _____ that I _____ would be dif - fer - ent. _____

my life is bet-ter; so is the world we're liv-ing in. I'm

thank-ful for the time I spent with my best friend.

(You're my best friend.)

Thank you for call - ing me out. Thank you for wak - ing me up.

Thank you for break - ing it ___ down. Thank you for choos - ing us. ___

Thank you for all you're a - bout. Thank you for lift - ing me up.

Thank you for keep - ing me ground - ed, ___ and be - ing here ___ now. ___

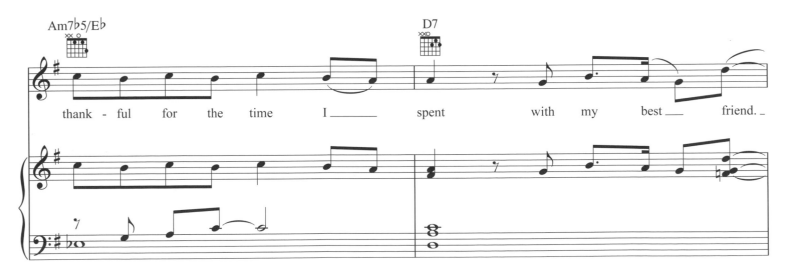

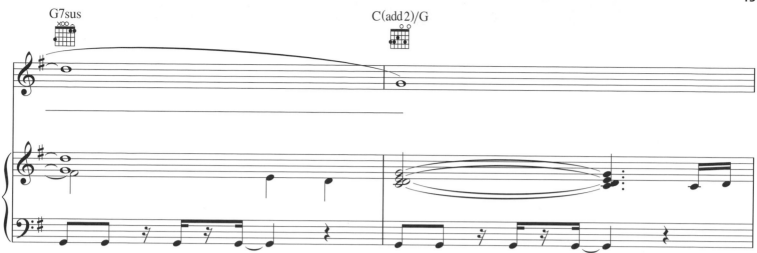

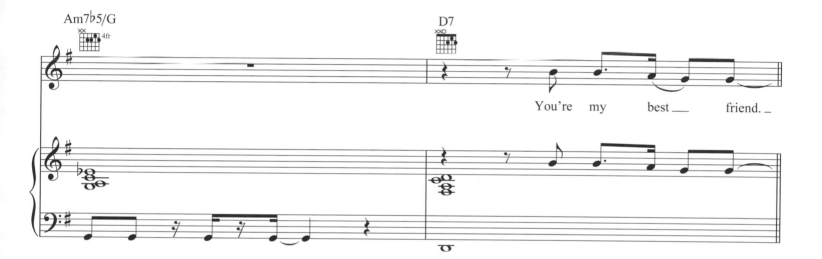

You're my best ___ friend. _

CAN'T HOLD OUT ON LOVE

Words and Music by JASON MRAZ
and MICHAEL HODGES

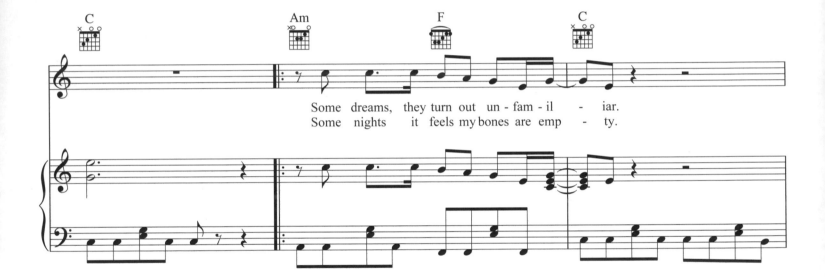

Some dreams, they turn out un-fam-il-iar.
Some nights it feels my bones are emp-ty.

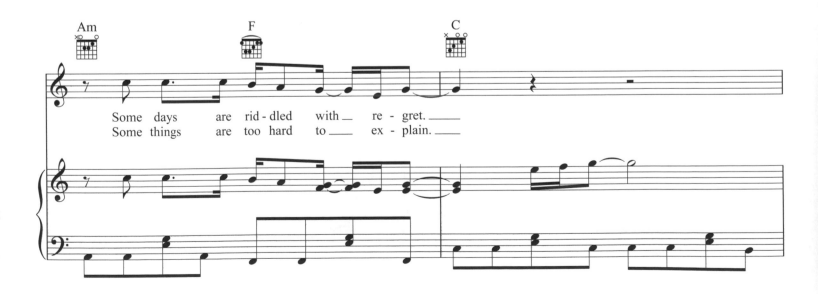

Some days are rid-dled with re-gret.
Some things are too hard to ex-plain.

And e-ven when_ you think_ it's o-ver,_____
Some-times I look_ at you_ with en-vy_____

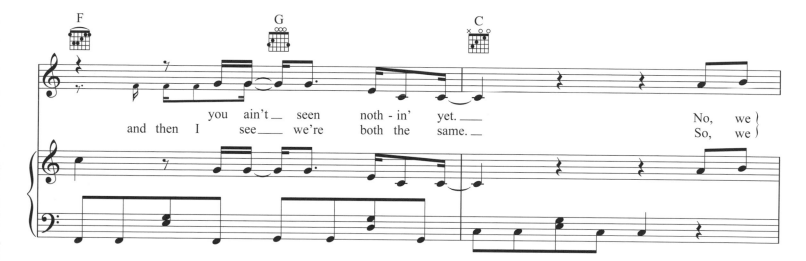

you ain't_ seen noth-in' yet. _____   No, we
and then I see_ we're both the same. _   So, we

can't hold out_____ on love. _   No, we can't hold out_ on love. _

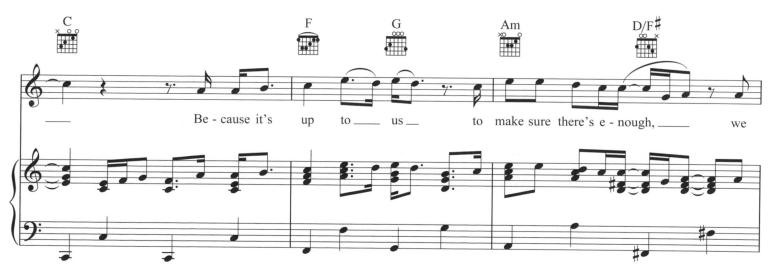

___ Be-cause it's up to_ us_ to make sure there's e-nough, _____ we

-'ry-bod-y breathes.___ All be-cause ___ all the love ___ ech-

-oes in the beat-ing of our hearts._____ Let's get ___ start-ed. You ___

can't hold ___ out ___ on love.___ No, we can't hold ___ out ___ on love.___

Be-cause it's up to ___ us ___ to

make sure there's e - nough, _____ we can't hold ___ out ___ on love. _____ No, we

can't hold ___ out ___ on ___ love. ___ Oh no, we can't hold ___ out ___ on love. _

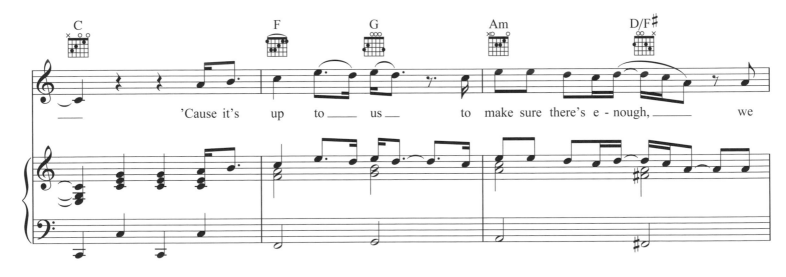

___ 'Cause it's up to ___ us ___ to make sure there's e - nough, _____ we

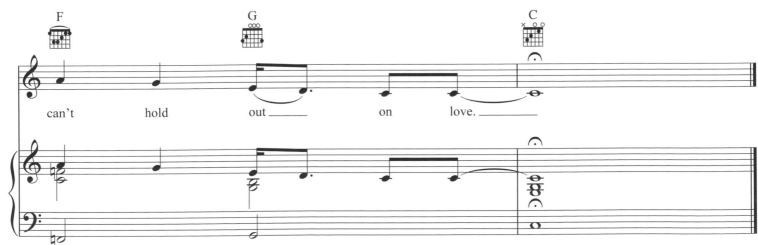

can't hold out _____ on love. _____

I'M YOURS

Words and Music by
JASON MRAZ

Moderately slow, with a Reggae feel

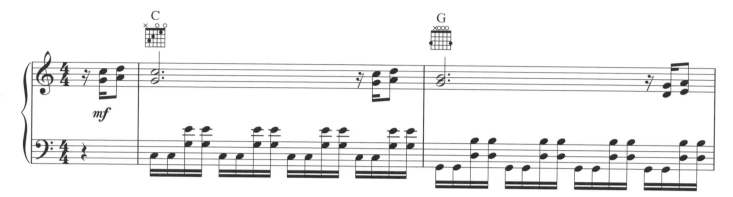

Well,

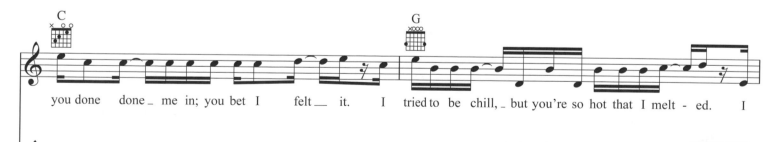

you done done me in; you bet I felt it. I tried to be chill, but you're so hot that I melt ed. I

Am **F**

fell right through the cracks. _____ Now I'm try-ing to get _ back. _____ Be-fore the

C **G**

cool done run out, I'll be giv-ing it my best - est, and noth-ing's gon-na stop me but di-vine in-ter-ven - tion. I

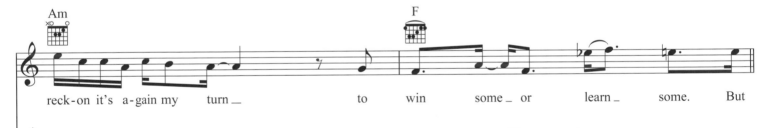

Am **F**

reck-on it's a-gain my turn _ to win some _ or learn _ some. But

C **G**

I _ won't hes - i - tate no more, _ no _____

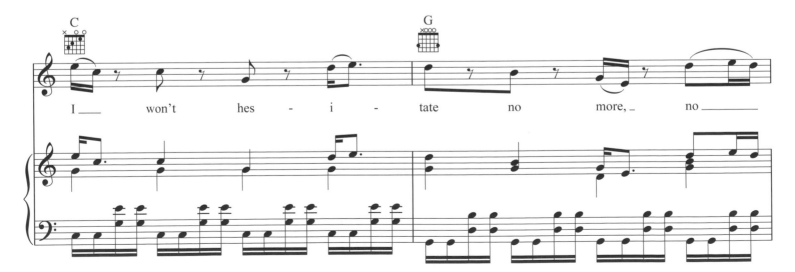

more. _ It can - not wait. I'm yours. _____

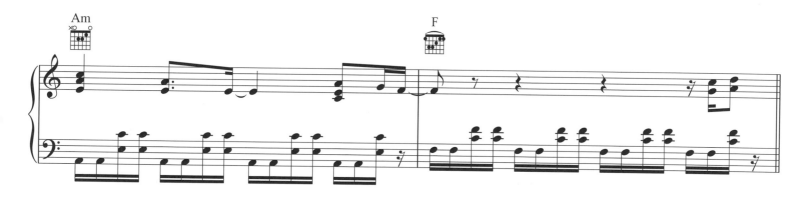

Well, o - pen up your mind and see _ like me. __ O - pen up your plans and, damn, _ you're free.

more. _ It can - not wait. I'm sure. _____ There's no

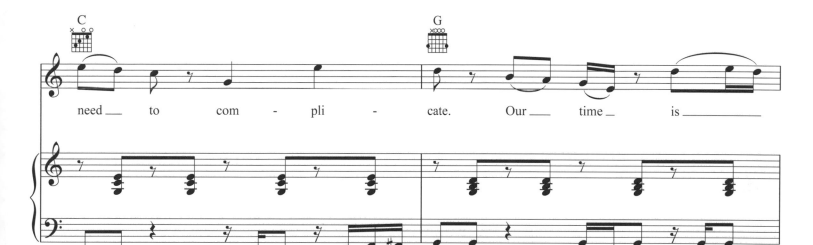

need ___ to com - pli - cate. Our ___ time ___ is _____

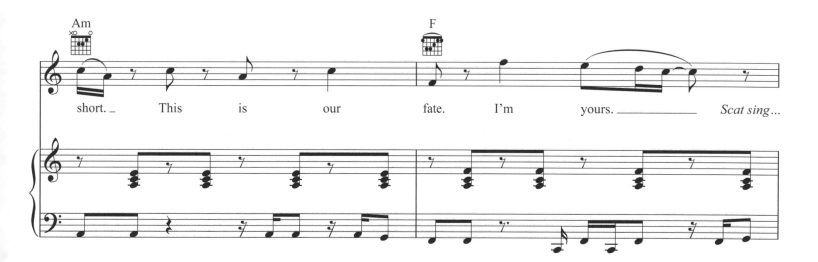

short. _ This is our fate. I'm yours. _____ *Scat sing...*

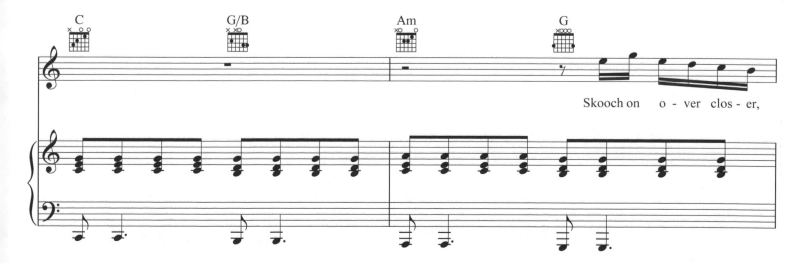

Skooch on o - ver clos - er,

dear, and I will nib-ble your ear. _____ *Scat sing...*

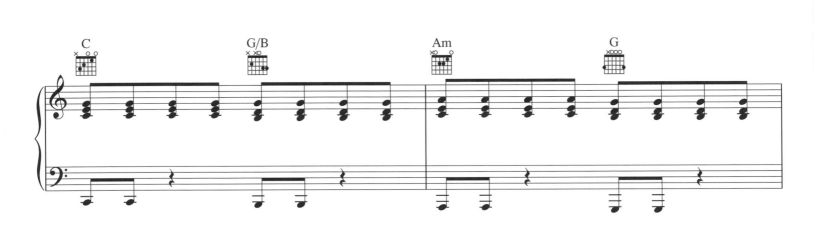

I've been spend-ing

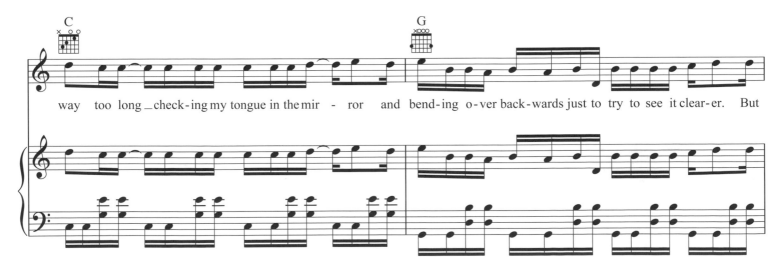

way too long _ check-ing my tongue in the mir - ror and bend-ing o-ver back-wards just to try to see it clear-er. But

Am   F

my breath fogged up the glass, and so I drew a new face and I laughed.   I

C   G

guess what I'll be say-ing is there ain't no bet-ter rea-son to rid your-self of van - i - ties and just go with the sea-sons. It's

Am   F

what we aim to do. Our name is our vir - tue. But

C   G

I won't hes - i - tate no more, no

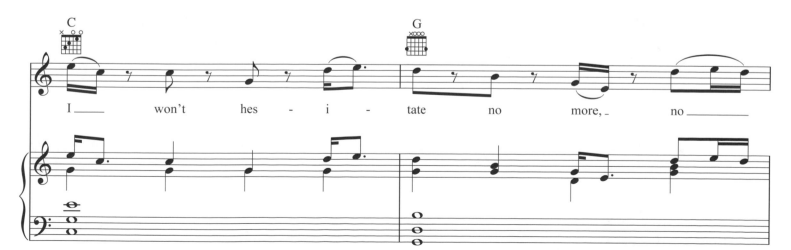

more. ___ It can - not wait. I'm yours. _____

O - pen up your mind ___ and see like ___ me. ___ O - pen up your plans ___ and, damn, ___ you're free. ___
(I won't hes - i - tate no more, no

___ Look in - to your heart ___ and you'll find ___ that ___ the sky ___ is yours. _____ So
more. It can - not ___ wait. I'm ___ sure. _____ No

please don't, please don't, please don't... There's no need to com - pli - cate 'cause our time

need to com - pli - cate. Our time is

_ is short. _ This is, this is, this is our fate. I'm yours. _ _ _ _ _ _ _ Scat sing...

short. This is our fate. I'm yours.) _ _ _ _ _ _ _

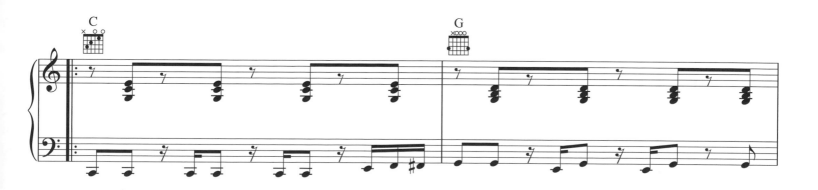

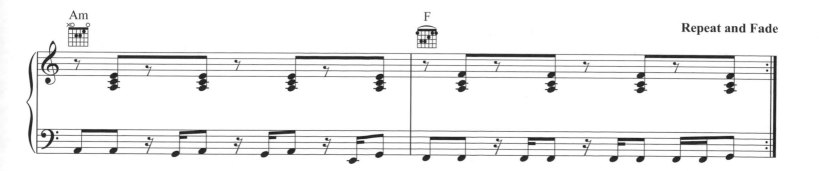

Repeat and Fade

DETAILS IN THE FABRIC
(Sewing Machine)

Words and Music by JASON MRAZ
and DAN WILSON

* *Recorded a half step lower.*

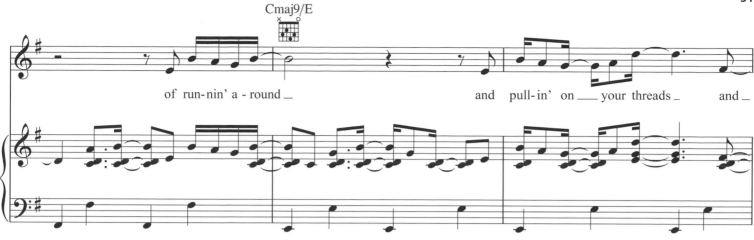

of run-nin' a - round ___ and pull-in' on ___ your threads ___ and ___

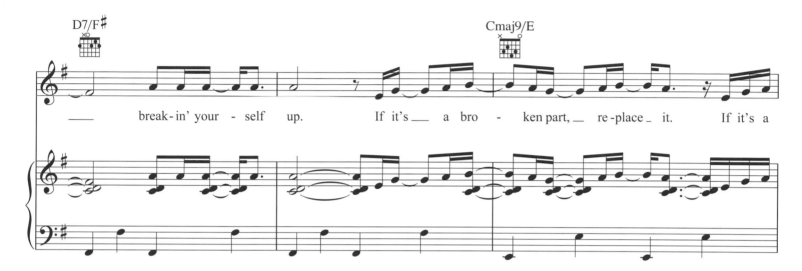

___ break-in' your - self up. If it's ___ a bro - ken part, ___ re -place ___ it. If it's a

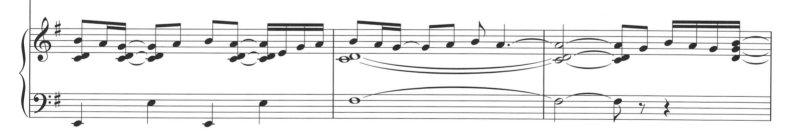

bro-ken arm ___ then brace it. If it's a bro-ken heart ___ then face it. And hold ___ your own, ___

know ___ your name ___ and go your own _____ way. ___

Hold _ your own, _ know _ your name _ and go your

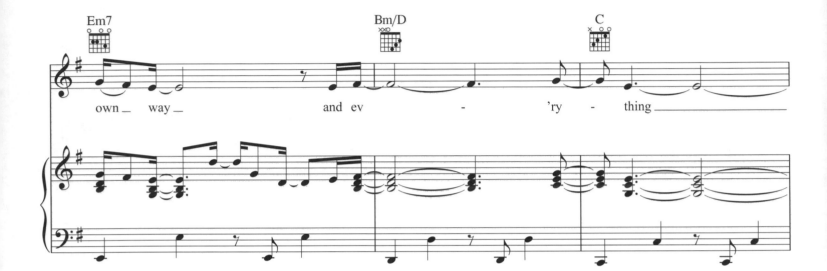

own _ way _ and ev - 'ry - thing _____

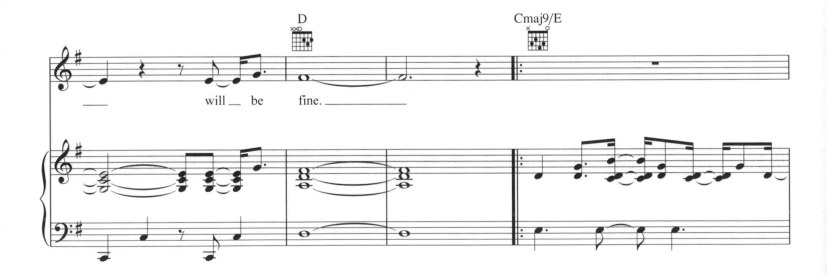

will _ be fine. _____

Hang _____ on, _____ help is on __

__ the way. __ Stay _____ strong, _____

__ I'm do-in' ____ ev - 'ry - thing. _____ Hold __ your own, __

__ know __ your name __ and go your own __ way. __

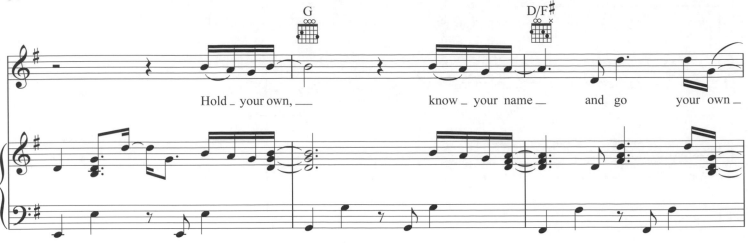

Hold _ your own, __ know _ your name _ and go your own _

__ way __ and ev - 'ry - thing, ev - 'ry -

thing will __ be fine, ev - 'ry - thing. Are the de -

- tails in the fab - ric? Are the things that make _ you pan - ic. Are your

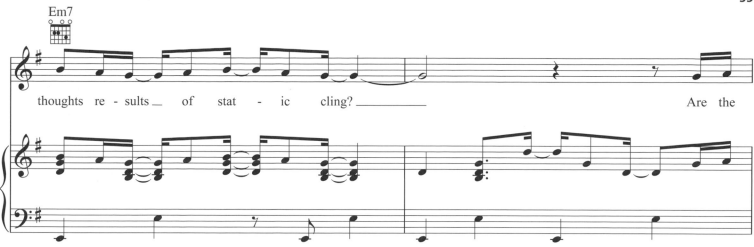

thoughts re - sults __ of stat - ic cling? _____ Are the

things that make you go, _____ for no rea - son, go out and scream. __ If you're

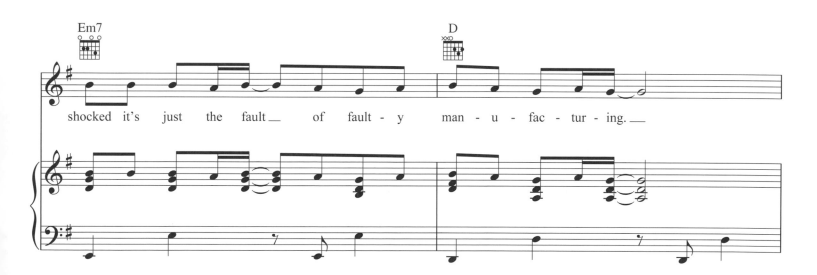

shocked it's just the fault __ of fault - y man - u - fac - tur - ing. __

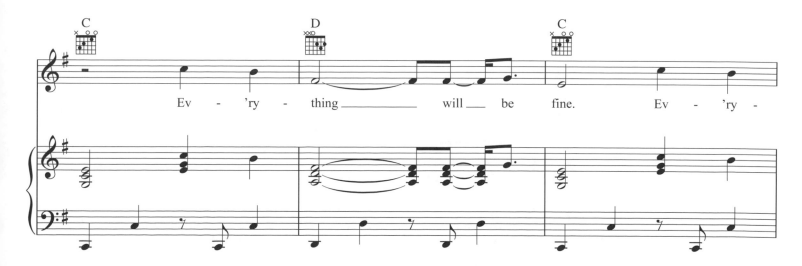

Ev - 'ry - thing _____ will __ be fine. Ev - 'ry -

Ev - 'ry - thing _____ will __ be fine. Ev - 'ry -

thing _____ in no __ time __ at all, __ hearts will hold. _____

Cmaj9/E

D7/F#

Repeat and Fade

Optional Ending

Cmaj9/E

HAVE IT ALL

Words and Music by JASON MRAZ,
JACOB KASHER HINDLIN, DAVID HODGES,
BECKY GEBHARDT, CHASKA POTTER,
MAI BLOOMFIELD and MONA TAVAKOLI

Half-time Shuffle feel

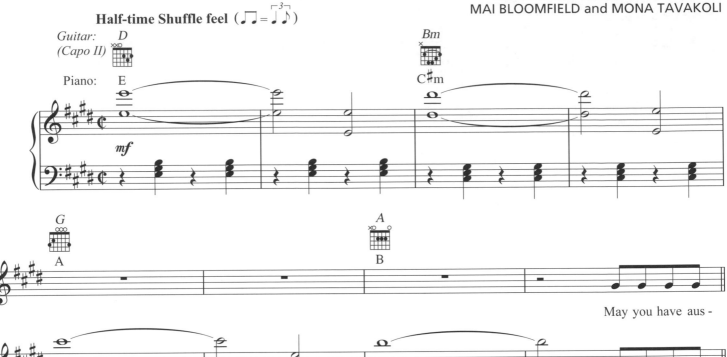

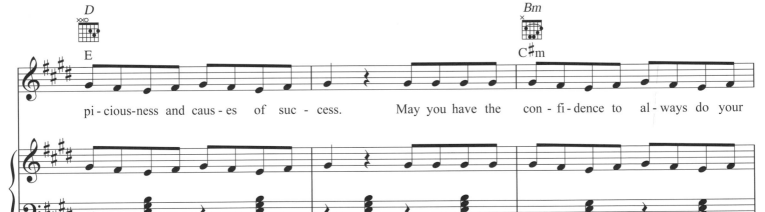

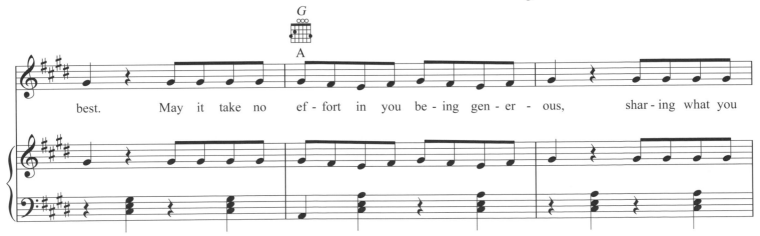

wealth. May you get a gold star on your next test. May your ed - u -

cat - ed guess - es al - ways be cor - rect. And may you win priz - es, shin - ing like

D.S. al Coda

dia - monds. May you real - ly own it each mo - ment to the next. And may the

CODA

Oh, _____ I want you to have it.

Oh, _____ all _____ you can i - mag - ine. Oh, _____ no

mat - ter what your path is, if you be - lieve it, then an - y - thing can hap - pen.

Go, go, go, raise your glass - es. Go, go, go,

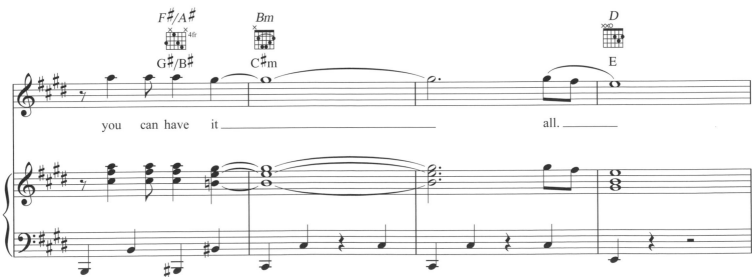

you can have it _____ all. _____

I WON'T GIVE UP

Words and Music by JASON MRAZ
and MICHAEL NATTER

*Guitarists: Tune 6th string down to D.

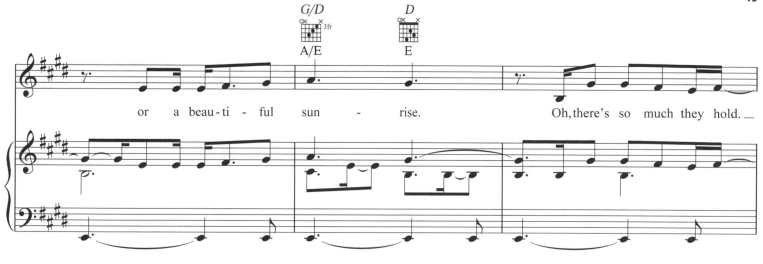

or a beau-ti-ful sun - rise. Oh, there's so much they hold. __

__ And just like them old __ stars,

I see that you've come so __ far __ to be right where __

you are. How old is your soul? __

Well, I won't give up ___ on us e - ven if the

skies ___ get ___ rough. __ I'm giv - ing ___ you all ___ my

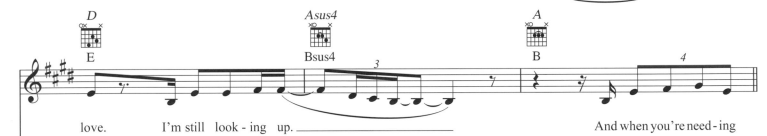

love. I'm still look - ing up. ___ And when you're need - ing

your space ___ to do some nav - i - gat - ing, ___

IF IT KILLS ME

Words and Music by JASON MRAZ,
MARTIN TEREFE and SACHA SKARBEK

such a beau-ti-ful mo - ment to see the look on your __ face,

to know that _____ I know that you know ___ now. _____

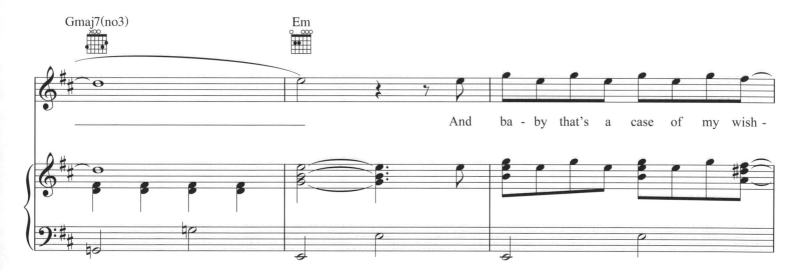

_____ And ba - by that's a case of my wish-

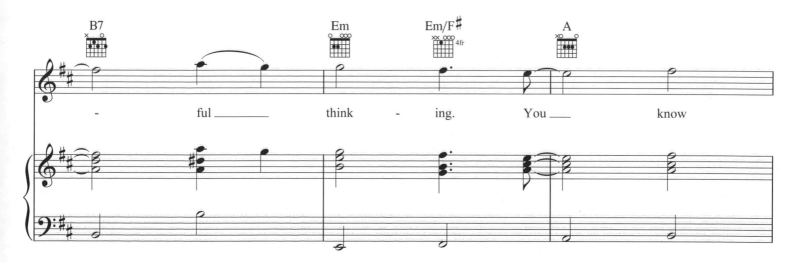

- ful _____ think - ing. You ___ know

noth - ing. Well, you and I, _____ why, we go ____ car -

- ry - in' on ____ for hours _____ on ____ end. _____ We get a - long____

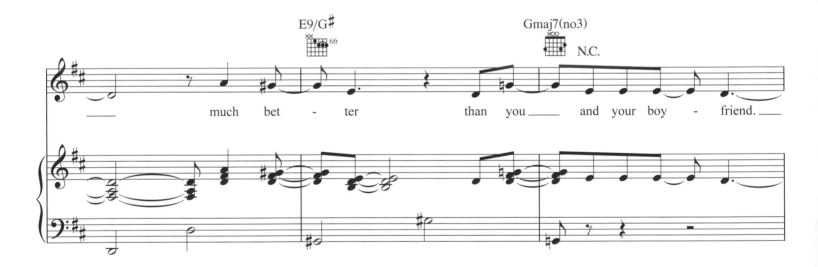

____ much bet - ter than you ____ and your boy - friend. ____

Well, all I real - ly wan - na do is a love____

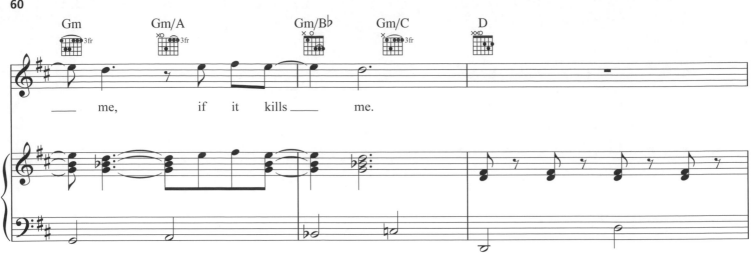

me, if it kills me.

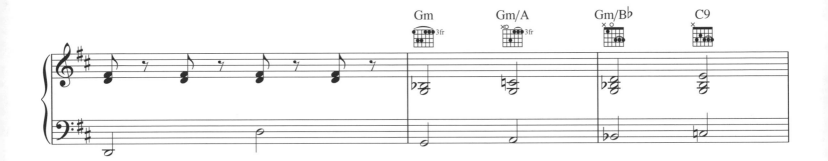

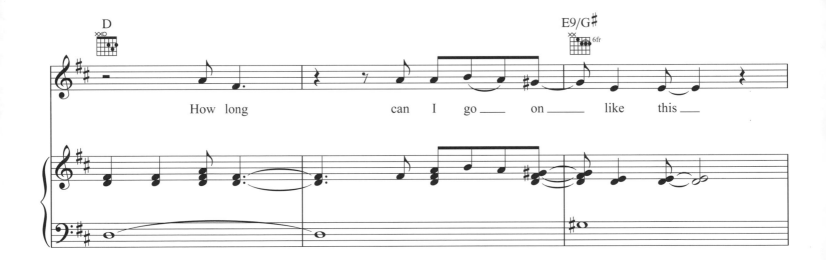

How long can I go on like this

wish - in' to kiss you be - fore I right - ly ex - plode?

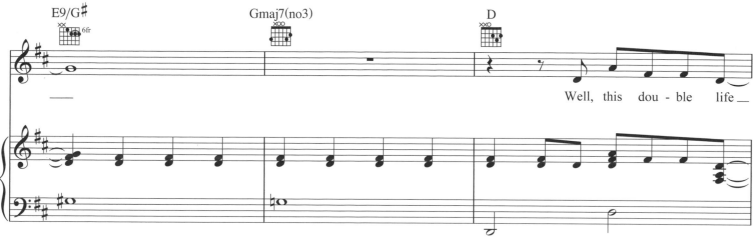

in _____ case I'm _____ wrong. _____

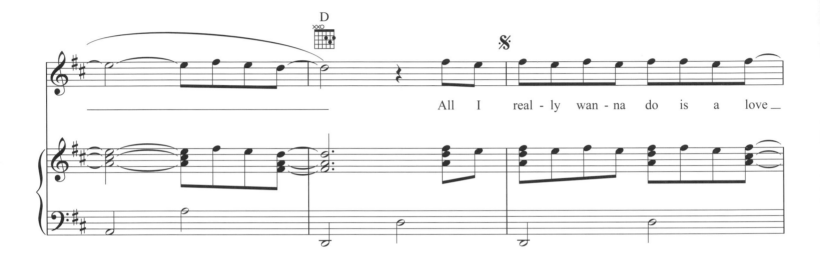

_____ All I real - ly wan - na do is a love _____

_____ you _____ a kind much clos - er than friends _____ use. _____ I

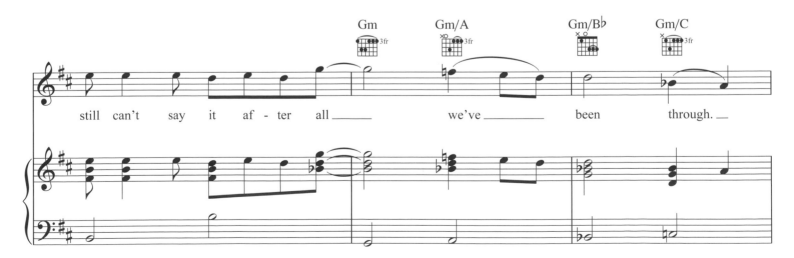

still can't say it af - ter all _____ we've _____ been _____ through. _____

And all I real-ly want from you is to feel___ me as the

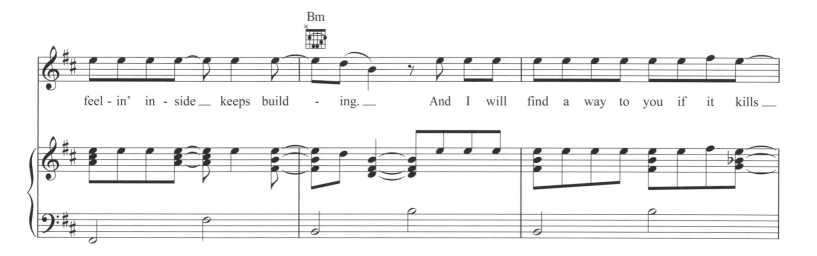

feel-in' in-side___ keeps build - ing.___ And I will find a way to you if it kills___

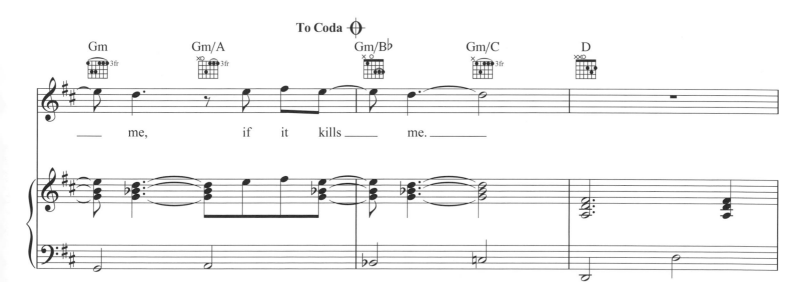

To Coda

___ me, if it kills ___ me. _____

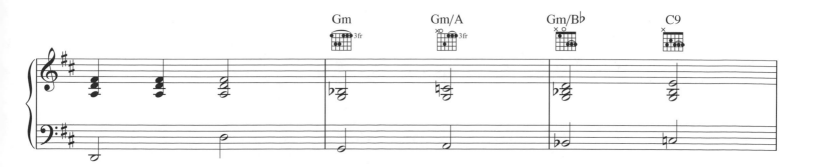

If I should be so bold, ___ I'd ask you to hold ___ my heart ___

___ in your hand. ___ I'll tell you from the start how I long ___ to be your man. ___

But I nev-er said a word. I guess I'm

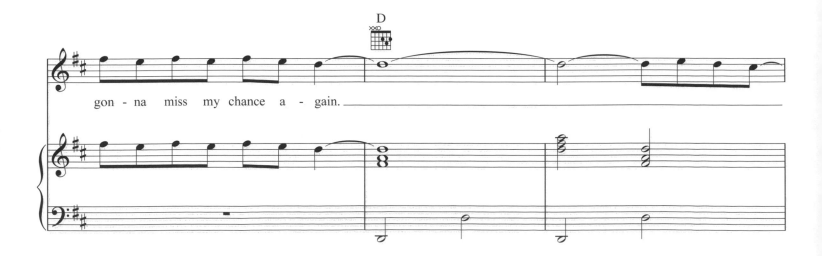

gon-na miss my chance a-gain. _____

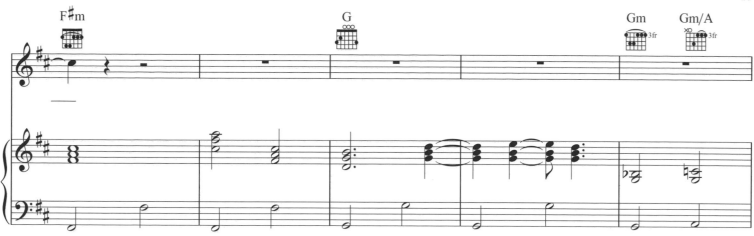

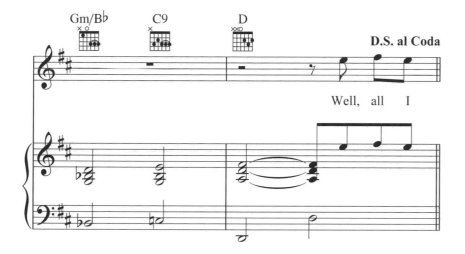

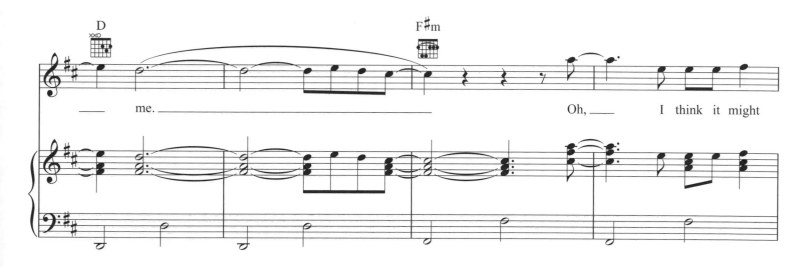

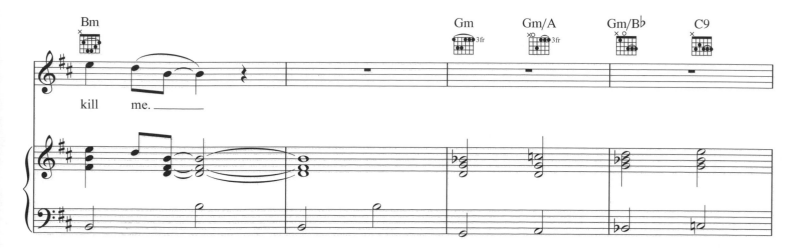

And all I real-ly wan-na do is a feel___ you. Yeah, the

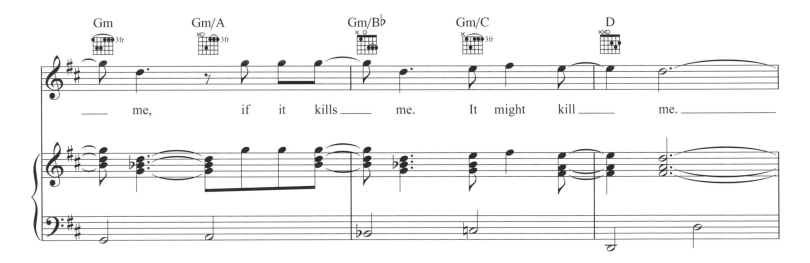

feel-in' in-side___ keeps build - ing. I'll find a way to you if it kills___

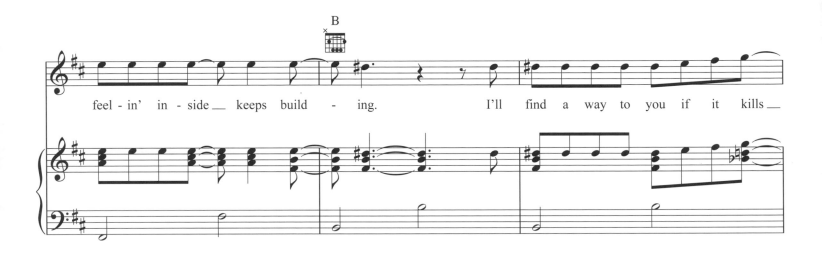

___ me, if it kills___ me. It might kill___ me.___

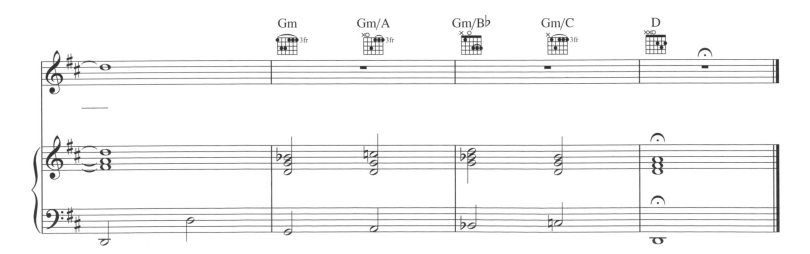

LIVING IN THE MOMENT

Words and Music by JASON MRAZ
and RICK NOWELS

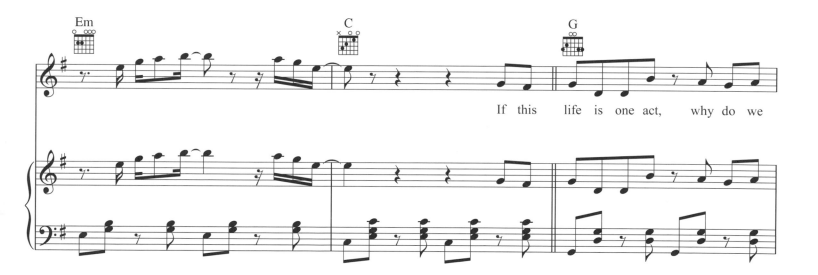

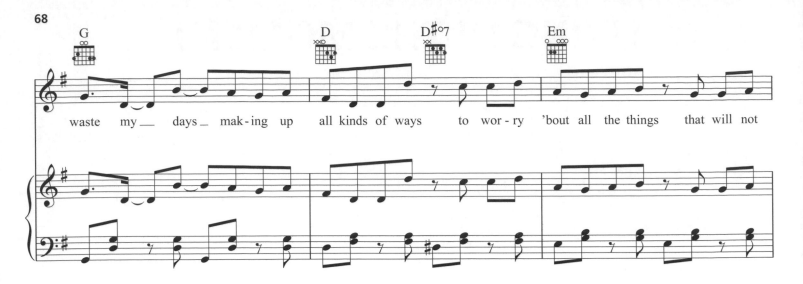

waste my __ days __ mak-ing up all kinds of ways to wor-ry 'bout all the things that will not

hap-pen to me. So I just let go of what I know I don't __ know. __ And I

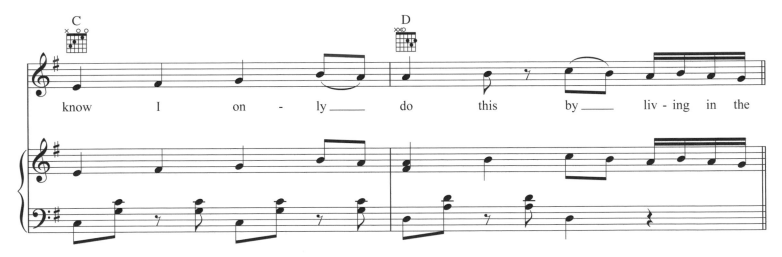

know I on - ly ____ do this by ____ liv-ing in the

mo - ment, __ liv-ing my life, __ eas - y and

breez - y with peace __ in my mind, with peace __ in my

heart, _____ with peace __ in my soul. _____ Wher-ev - er I'm __

go - ing, _____ I'm al - read-y home. __ Liv - ing in the

mo - ment. I'm let-ting my-self __ off __ the hook for

things I've __ done. I let my past go __ past, and now I'm hav- ing more fun. I'm let- ting

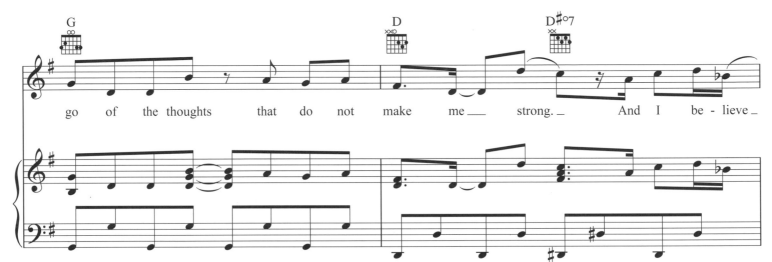

go of the thoughts that do not make me __ strong. __ And I be- lieve __

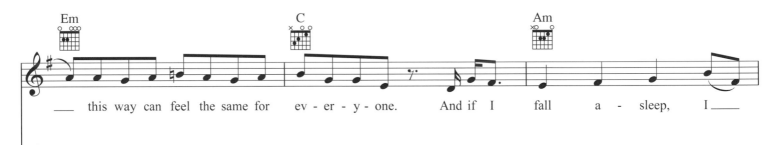

__ this way can feel the same for ev- er- y- one. And if I fall a- sleep, I __

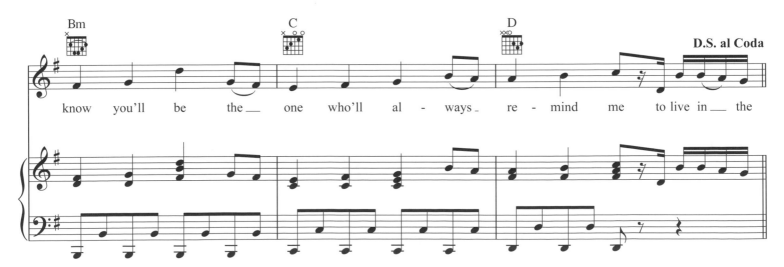

know you'll be the __ one who'll al- ways __ re- mind me to live in __ the

D.S. al Coda

CODA

go - ing, _____ I'm al - read - y home. _____ I can't

walk through life _____ fac - ing back - wards. ____

I have tried. ___ I tried ___ more than once to just ___ make sure, ___ and

I _____ was de - nied _____ the fu - ture I'd ____ been search - ing for. ___ I

go - ing, _____ I'm al - read - y home. _____ I'm a liv - ing in the

I'm let - ting

mo - ment. _____ I'm a liv - ing my life, _____ just tak - in' it _____

my - self _____ off _____ the hook for things I've _____ done. _____ I let my

eas - y _____ with peace _____ in my mind. _____ Got peace _____ in my

past go _____ past, and now I'm hav - ing more fun. I'm let - ting

heart. _____ Got peace __ in my soul. _____ Wher-ev-er I'm __

go of the thoughts that do not make me __ strong. __ And I be-

go - ing, ___ I'm al-read-y home. _____ I'm - a liv-ing in the

lieve this way can feel the same for ev-er-y-one. I'm let-ting

mo - ment. __ I'm - a liv-ing my life, _____ eas - y and

my-self __ off __ the hook for things I've __ done. __ I let my

LOVE SOMEONE

Words and Music by JASON MRAZ, BECKY GEBHARDT,
MAI SUNSHINE BLOOMFIELD, CHASKA POTTER,
MONA TAVAKOLI, CHRIS KEUP
and STEWART MYERS

whole heart as my heart re - ceives your

love.
time.

Oh, ain't ___ it nice to - night ___ we've got ___ each oth -
Oh, ain't ___ it nice ___ this life ___ we've got ___ each oth -

- er? ___
- er? ___

And I am

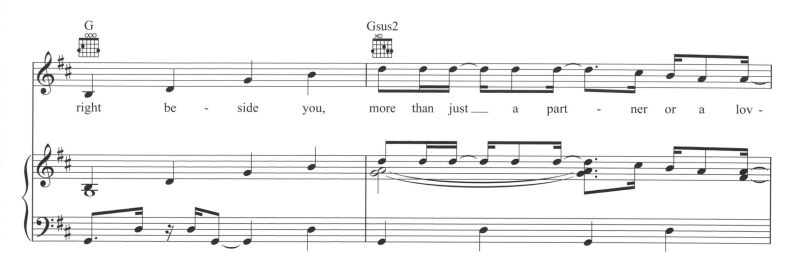

right be - side you, more than just ___ a part - ner or a lov -

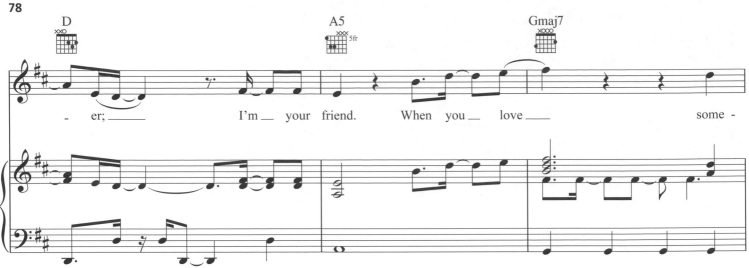

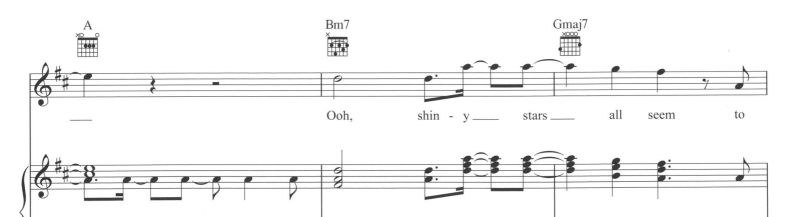

To Coda ⊕

con - gre - gate ___ a - round ___ your face. When you love ___ some -

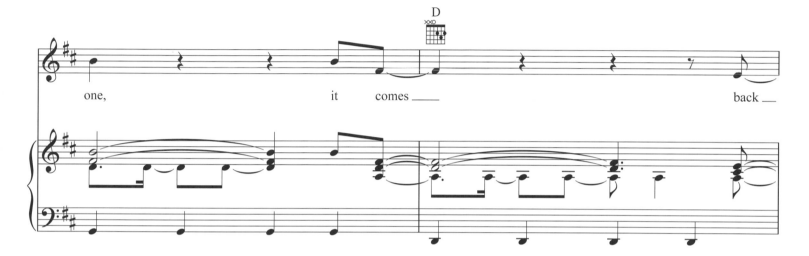

one, ___ it comes ___ back ___

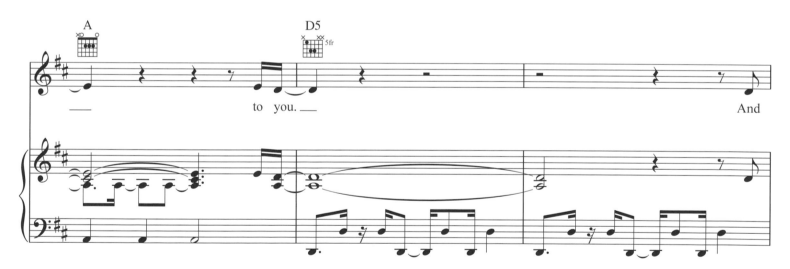

to you. ___ And

love ___ is a fun - ny thing; ___ it's mak - ing my

blood flow with en - er - gy. _____ And this

life, an a - wak - ing _____ dream, is what I've been

D.S. al Coda

wish - ing for is hap - pen - ing. _____ And it's right on

CODA

A

one, when _ you love some - one...

We're gon - na give __ our - selves __ to love __ to - night, __

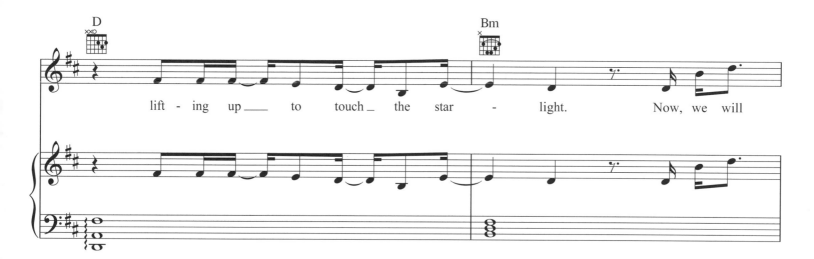

lift - ing up __ to touch __ the star - light. Now, we will

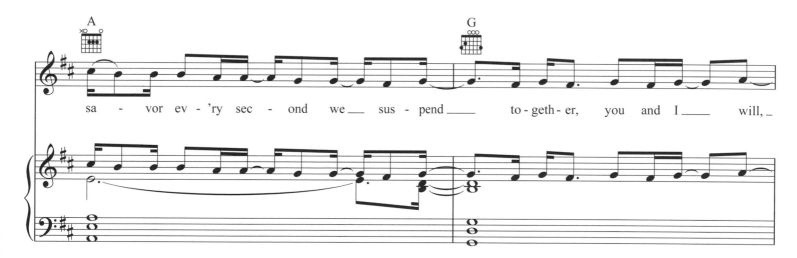

sa - vor ev - 'ry sec - ond we __ sus - pend __ to - geth - er, you and I __ will, __

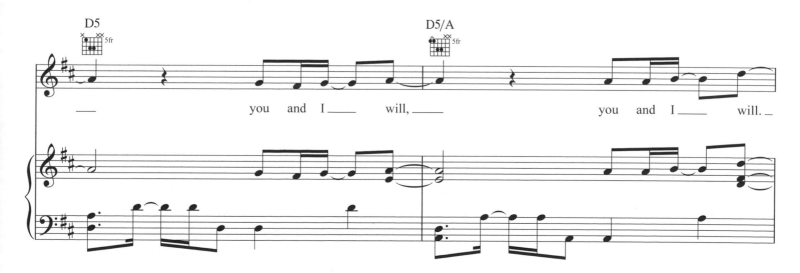

__ you and I __ will, __ you and I __ will. __

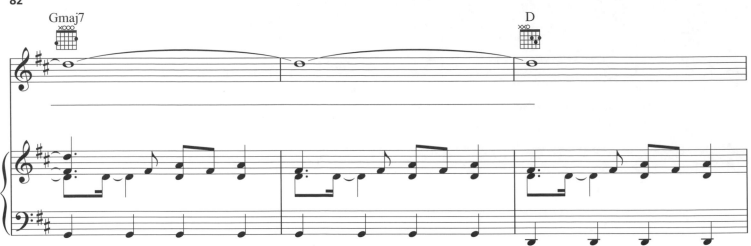

When you ___ love _____ some -

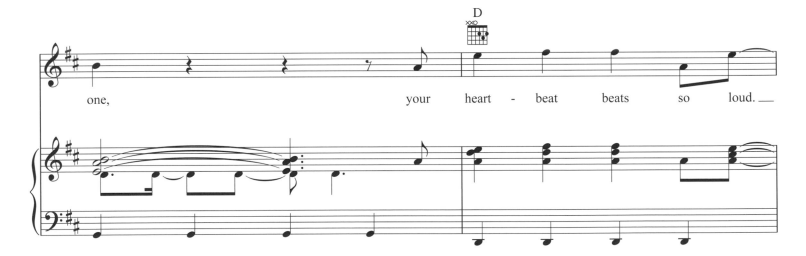

one, your heart - beat beats so loud. ___

___ When you ___ love _____ some -

one, your feet can't feel the ground. _

Ooh, shin - y ___ stars ___ all seem to con - gre - gate ___ a - round ___

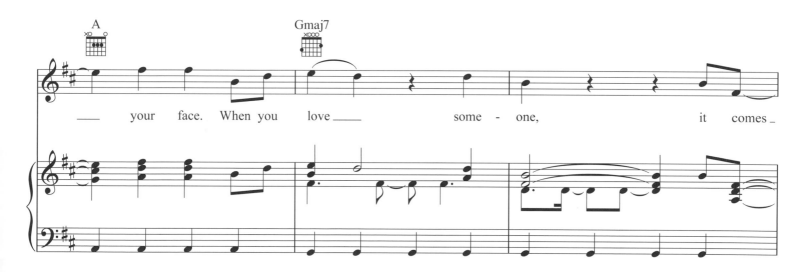

___ your face. When you love ___ some - one, it comes _

___ back ___ to you. ___

LUCKY

Words and Music by JASON MRAZ,
COLBIE CAILLAT and TIMOTHY FAGAN

Female vocal sung one octave lower than written.

*Substitute half rest on D.S.

MIGHT AS WELL DANCE

Words and Music by
JASON MRAZ

Moderate Country, in 2

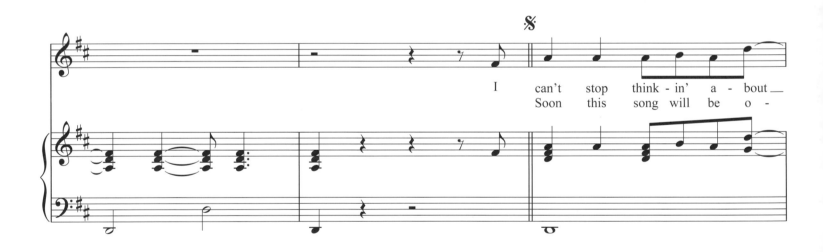

I can't stop think-in' a-bout ___
Soon this song will be o-

___ ya ___ and dream-in' of ___ your smile. I
-ver, we'll have to say ___ good - night.

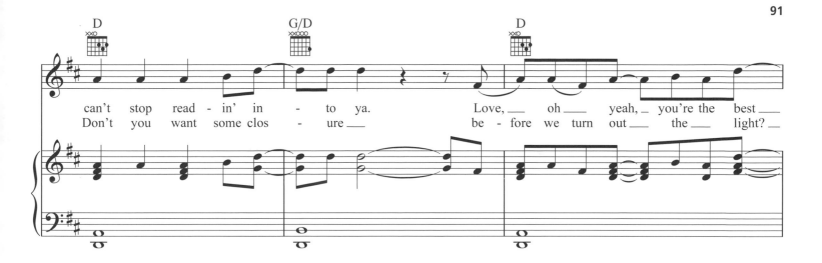

can't stop read - in' in - to ya. Love, __ oh __ yeah, _ you're the best __

Don't you want some clos - ure __ be - fore we turn out __ the __ light? __

__ book I read in a while. __ I don't just

__ Hon - ey, think of your heart. __ Yeah, _ the

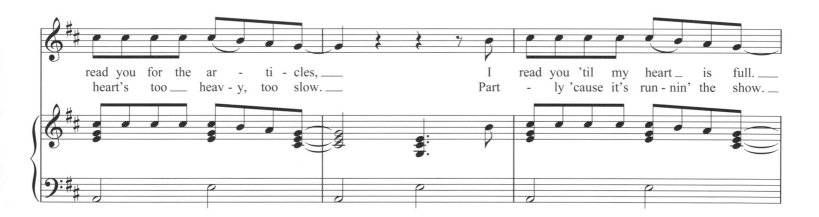

read you for the ar - ti - cles, __ I read you 'til my heart _ is full. __

heart's too __ heav - y, too slow. __ Part - ly 'cause it's run - nin' the show. __

__ You keep my heart a beat - in', you're keep - in' me from sleep - in'. The

__ Part - ly 'cause the beat is con - nect - ed to the feet and I've __

on-ly one I'm cheat-in' is me _____ if I don't take con-trol. _____
_____ got _____ the sweet-est _____ crush _____ on you, ba-by, let's go. _____

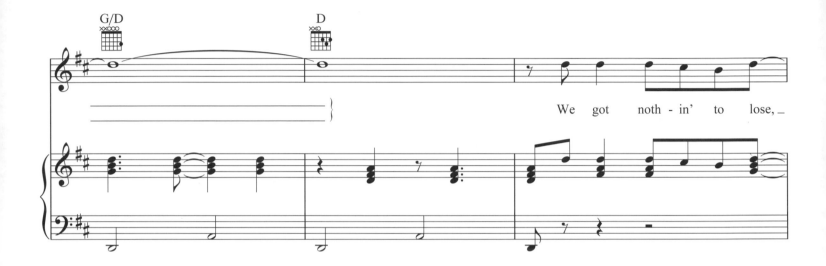

We got noth-in' to lose, _

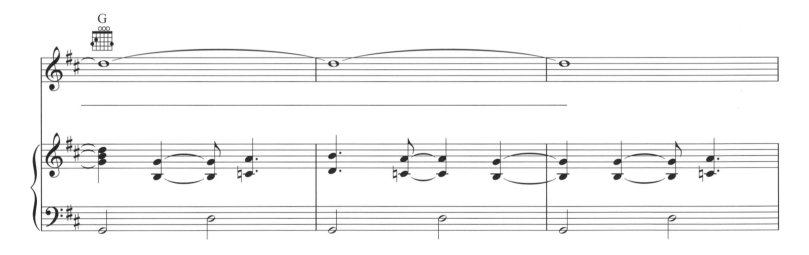

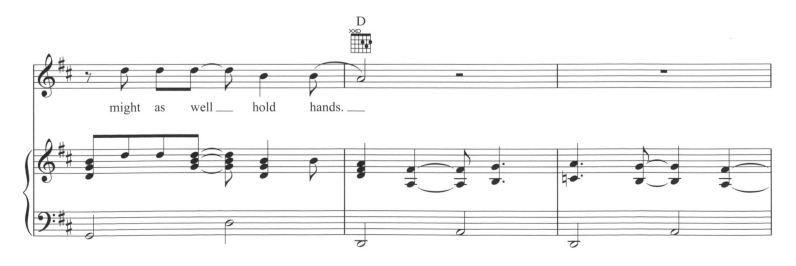

might as well _____ hold hands. _____

Yeah, we're al-read-y fools ____

so we might as well dance. ____

To Coda ⊕

Put your lov-in' arms ____ a-round ____ me once more ____

and we'll go crash - in' in - to folks __

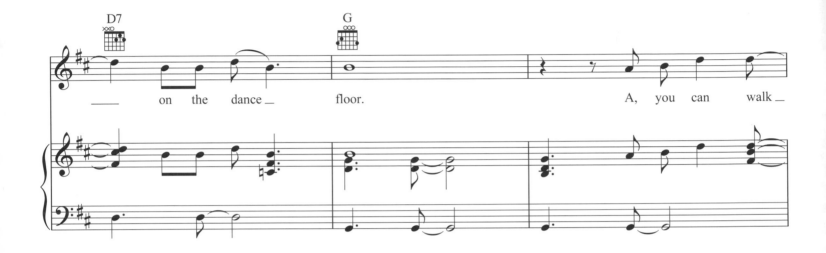

__ on the dance __ floor. A, you can walk __

__ all o - ver my shoes __ if you want to. __

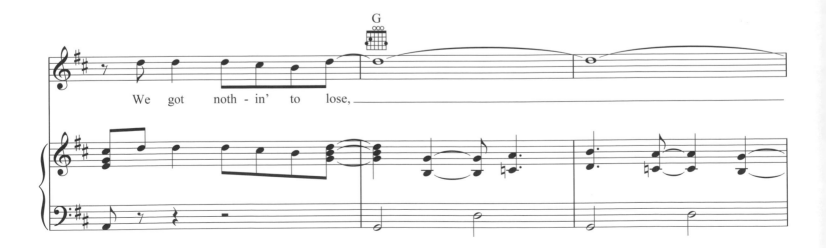

We got noth - in' to lose, __

might as well take off our pants. ___

Yeah, we're al - read - y fools ___

___ so we might as well dance. ___

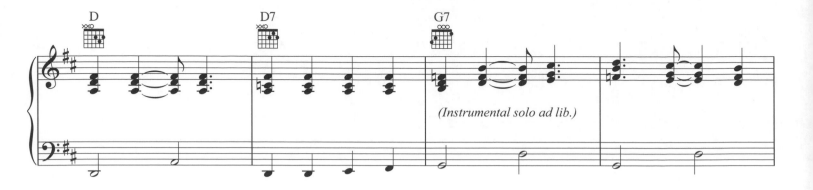

(Instrumental solo ad lib.)

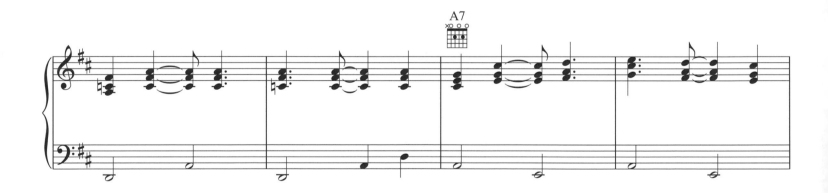

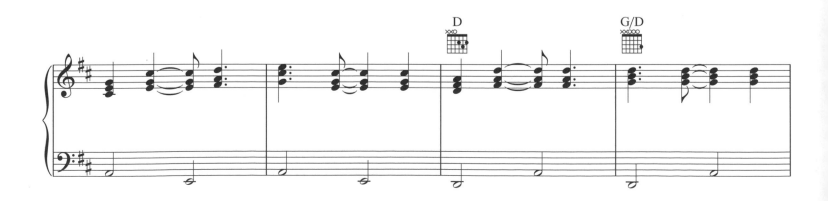

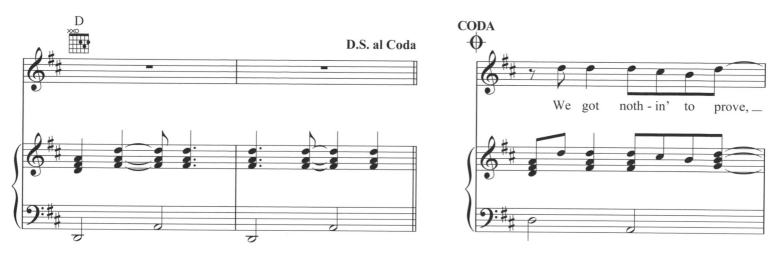

Yeah, we're al-read-y fools

so we might as well dance.

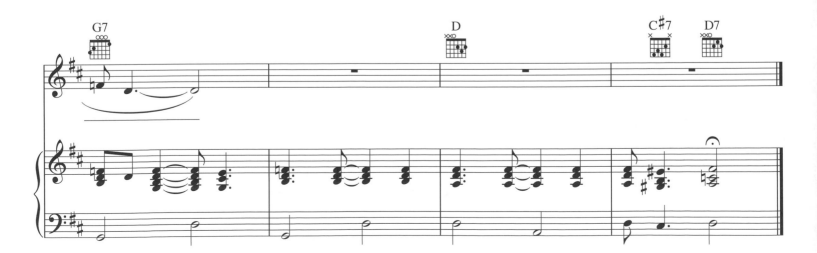

THE REMEDY
(I Won't Worry)

Words and Music by GRAHAM EDWARDS,
SCOTT SPOCK, LAUREN CHRISTY
and JASON MRAZ

Moderately, with a beat

Well, I ___ saw fire-
Well, I ___ heard two ___

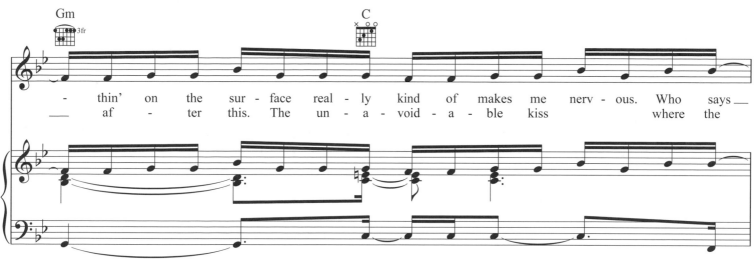

Gm — **C**

-thin' on the sur - face real - ly kind of makes me nerv - ous. Who says ___

___ af - ter this. The un - a - void - a - ble kiss where the

F — **Bb**

___ that you de - serve this and what kind of God would serve this? We will

mint - y fresh ___ bad ___ breath is sure to out - last ___ this ca -

Gm — **C** — **F** — N.C.

cure this dirt - y old ___ dis - ease. ___ Well, if } you've gots the poi - son, I've ___ gots the rem - e - dy. The

tas - tro - phe, dance ___ with me. ___ 'Cause if

Gm — **C** — **F** — **Bb**

rem - e - dy ___ is the ex - per - i - ence. This is a dan - ger - ous ___ li - ai - son. I ___ says, the

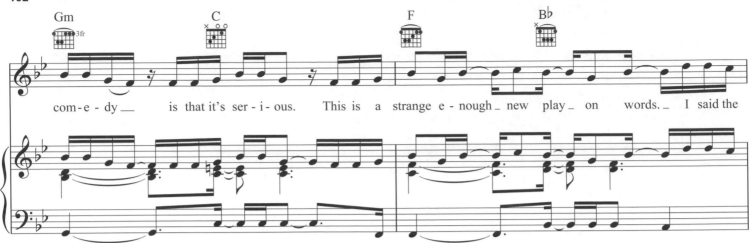

com-e-dy __ is that it's ser-i-ous. This is a strange e-nough __ new play __ on words. __ I said the

trag-e-dy is how you're gon-na __ spend __ the rest __ of your nights __ with the light __ on. So shine the

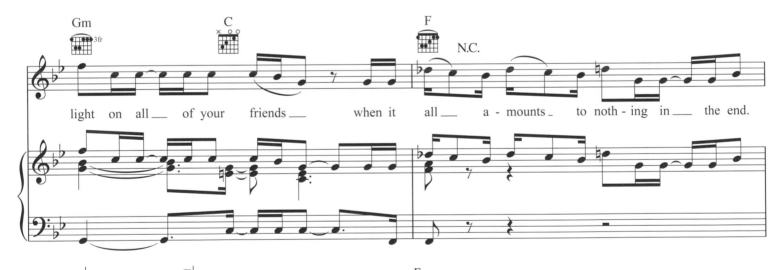

light on all __ of your friends __ when it all __ a-mounts __ to noth-ing in __ the end.

I, _____ I won't wor-ry my life __

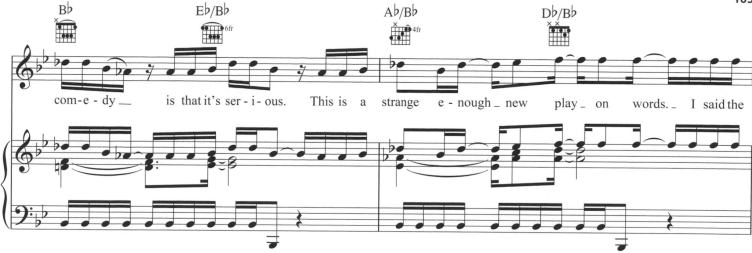

com-e-dy __ is that it's ser-i-ous. This is a strange e-nough __ new play __ on words. __ I said the

trag-e-dy is how you're gon-na __ spend __ the rest __ of your nights __ with the light __ on. So shine the

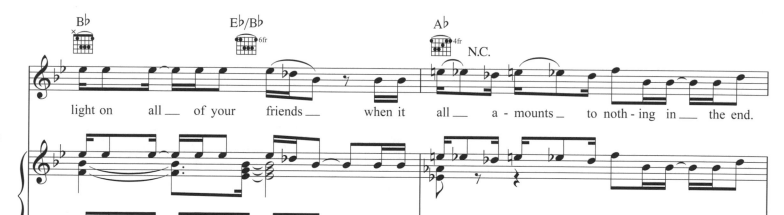

light on all __ of your friends __ when it all __ a-mounts __ to noth-ing in __ the end.

I, _____ I won't wor-ry my life __

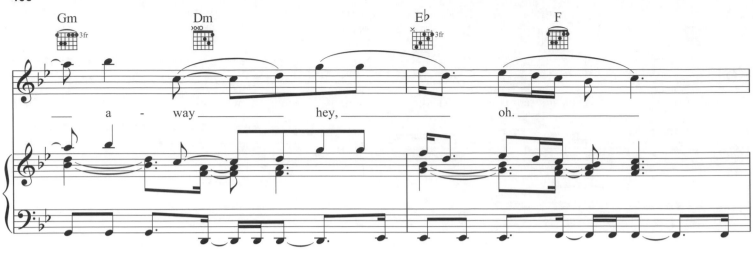

a - way _____ hey, _____ oh. _____

I, _____ I won't wor - ry my life _____

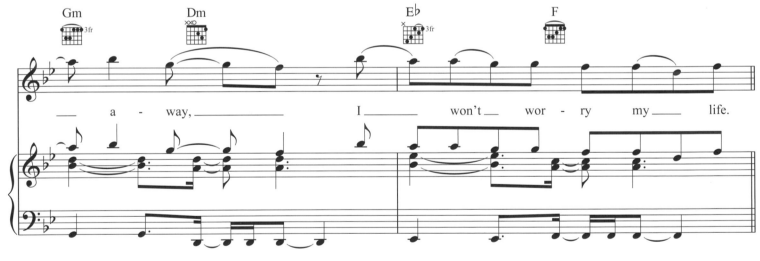

_____ a - way, _____ I _____ won't _____ wor - ry my _____ life.

I, _____ I won't wor - ry my life _____

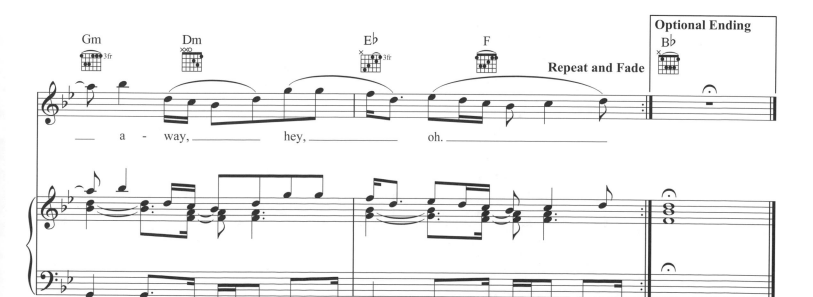

93 MILLION MILES

Words and Music by JASON MRAZ,
MICHAEL NATTER and MIKE DALY

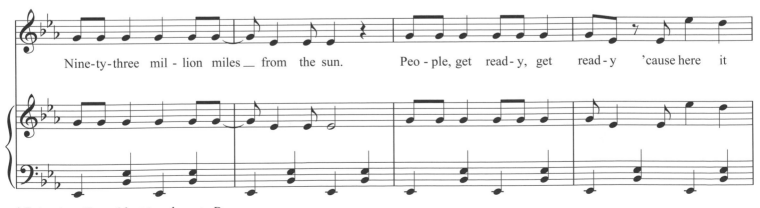

Nine-ty-three mil-lion miles __ from the sun. Peo-ple, get read-y, get read-y 'cause here it

*Guitarists: Tune 6th string down to D.

SLEEPING TO DREAM

Words and Music by JASON MRAZ
and PETER STUART

Moderate Folk

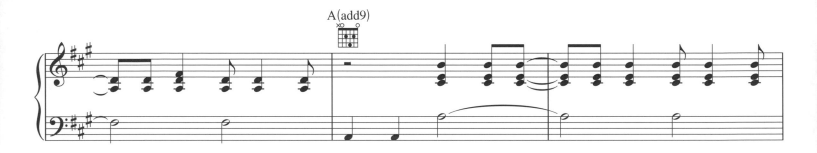

dream-in' of sleep - in' next ____ to you. I'm feel - in' like a lost lit - tle boy in a

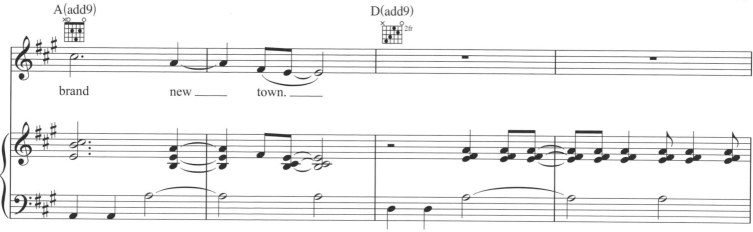

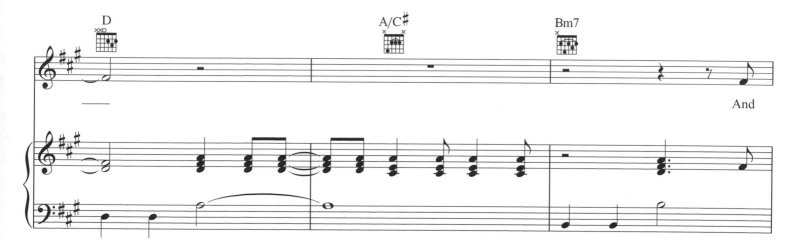

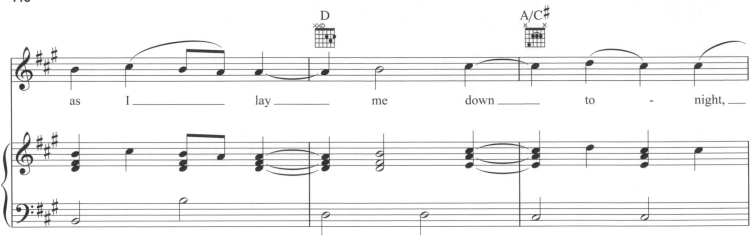

as I _____ lay _____ me down _____ to - night, _____

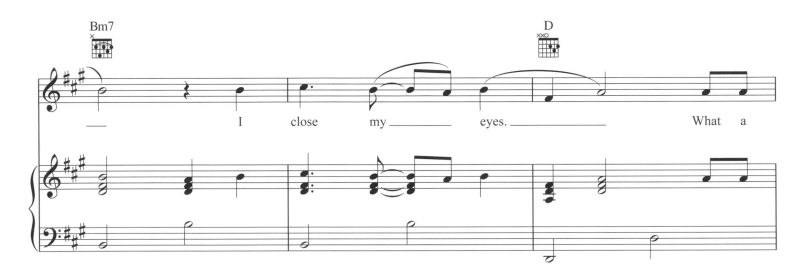

_____ I close my _____ eyes. _____ What a

beau - ti - ful ___ sight. _____ I'm sleep - in' to dream _ a - bout ___

___ you. I'm so _____ damn _____ tired _____ of

hav-in' to live __ with-out __ you __ but I, I __ don't mind. __

__ I'm sleep-in' to dream __ a-bout __ you.

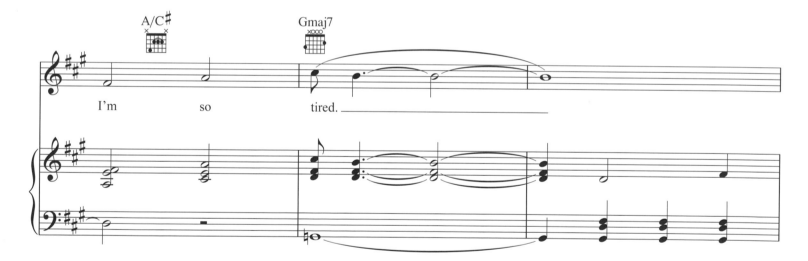

I'm so tired. __

Oh, __ yes I __

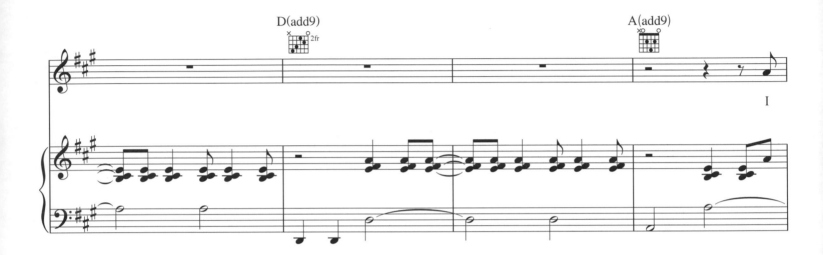

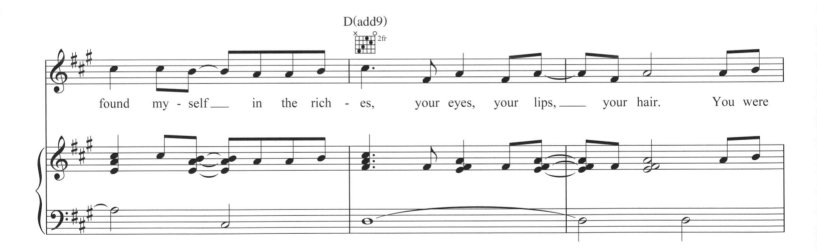

But I woke up in ___ the ditch - es, ___ I hit the light and I

thought you might be here but you were no - where. _____ Oh love, ___

___ you were no - where at ___ home. _____ And

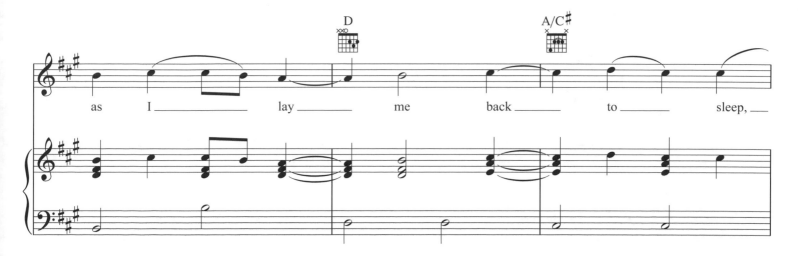

as I _____ lay _____ me back _____ to _____ sleep, ___

this love I ___ pray _____ that

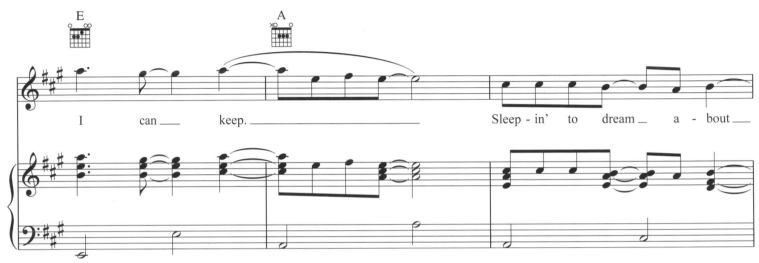

I can ___ keep. _____ Sleep - in' to dream ___ a - bout ___

___ you. I'm so ___ damn ___ tired ___ of

hav - in' to live ___ with - out _____ you _____ but I, _____ I don't ___

mind. I'm sleep - in' to dream __ a - bout __ you.

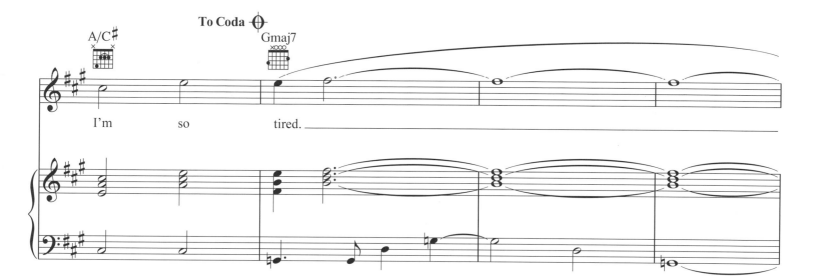

I'm so tired. ____

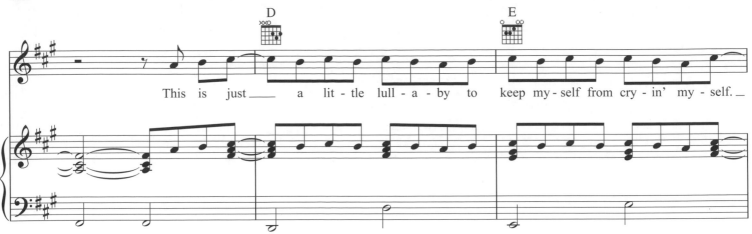

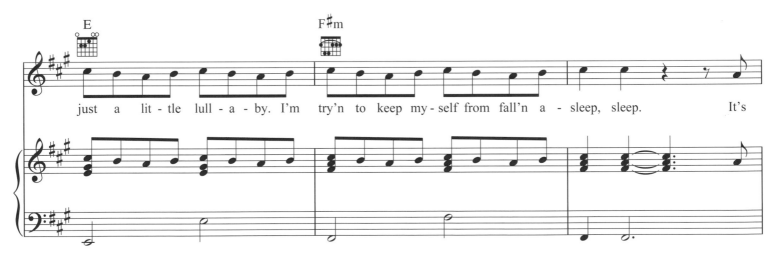

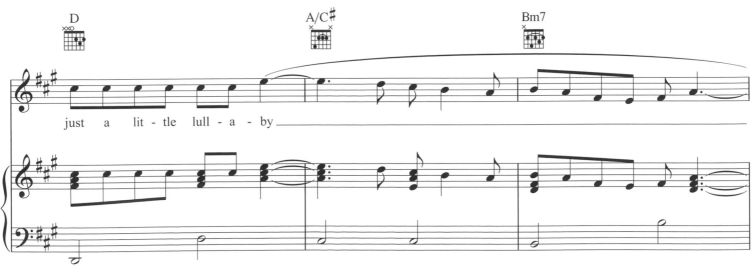

So I don't cry my - self ____ to sleep ____ at night. ____

D.S. al Coda

____ Sleep - in' to dream ____ a - bout ____

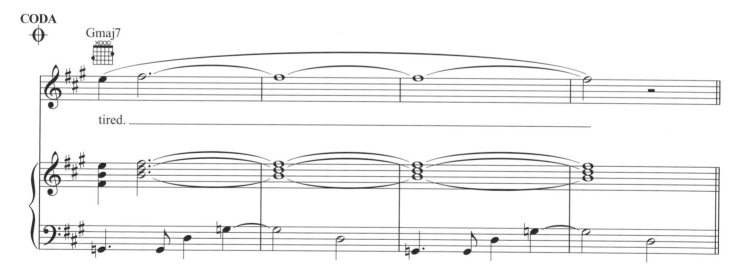

CODA

Gmaj7

tired. ____

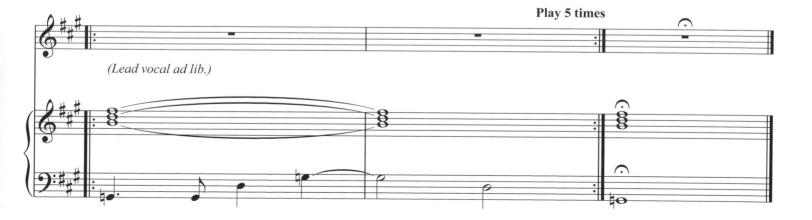

Play 5 times

(Lead vocal ad lib.)

UNLONELY

Words and Music by JASON MRAZ,
EMILY SCHWARTZ, SCOTT HARRIS
and ANDREW WELLS

lone - ly. We could take it slow - ly, and we could keep it

low - key. I could be your one and on - ly, I ___ could make you un -

lone - ly. I've been chas - ing sum - mer a - round, ___ search - ing for the sun - shine,

look - ing for a good time, fol - low - ing the good vibes, lis - ten - ing to in - tu - i - tion when it's hap - pen - ing.

dig-ging in-to life 'cause at times, __ it can be sad-den-ing. Yeah, it could be a gray day if you're lone-ly.

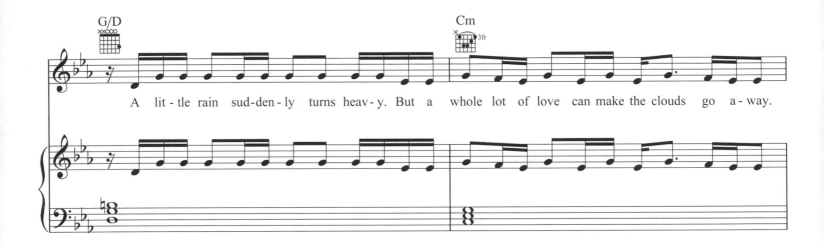

A lit-tle rain sud-den-ly turns heav-y. But a whole lot of love can make the clouds go a-way.

May-be the time __ for us is ___ now. When the ta-ble's set for two and there's

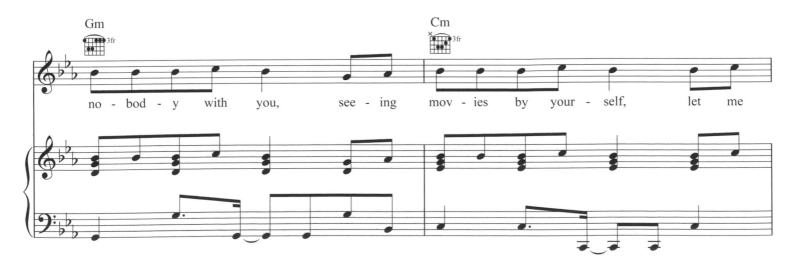

no-bod-y with you, see-ing mov-ies by your-self, let me

one and on - ly, I ___ could make you un - lone - ly.   Love,   la la la la

la. ___   Love,   la la la.

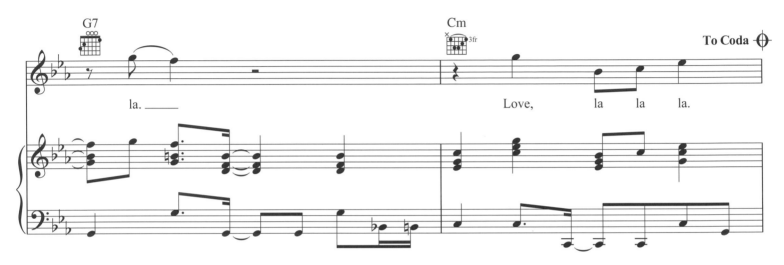

One   and on - ly, I ___ could make you un - lone ___ ly.
                                           I   give you my word, ___ al - though I'm mak - ing words   up. Un -

lone - ly ain't a word, but I ___ don't give a fuck. 'Cause I'm fresh from the farm where crit - ics can't both - er me.

WORDPLAY

Words and Music by JASON MRAZ
and KEVIN KADISH

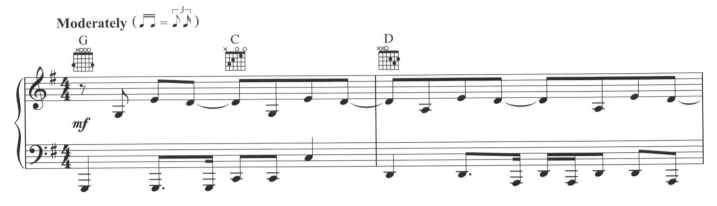

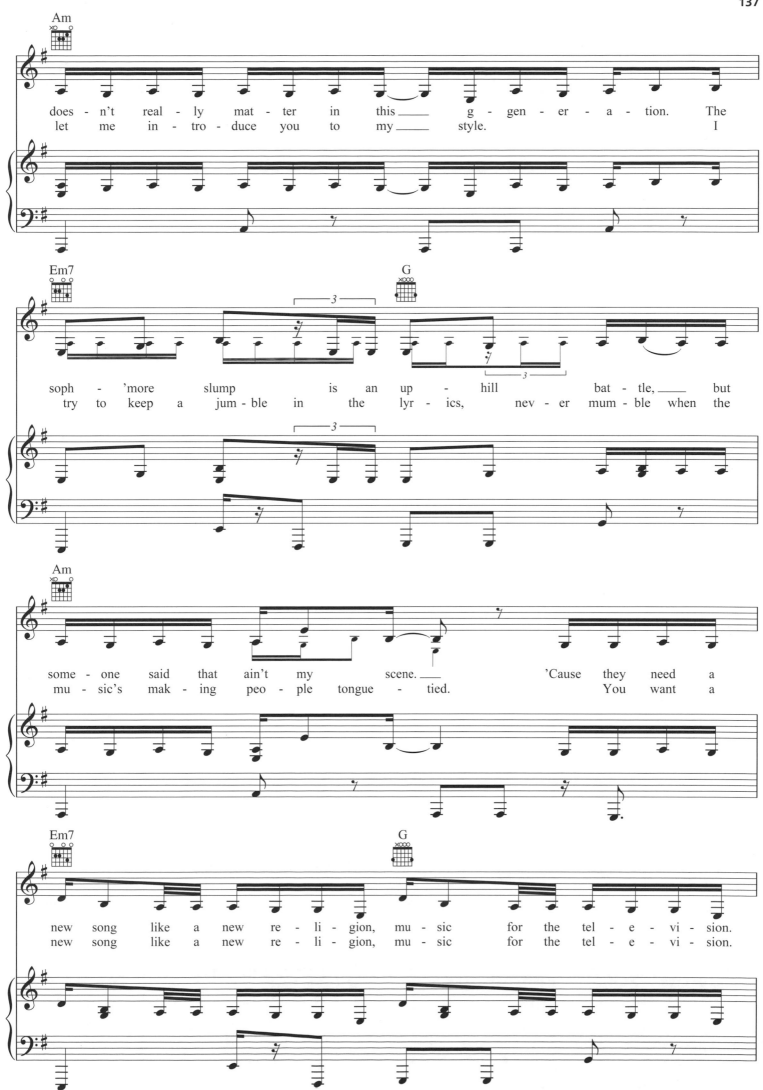

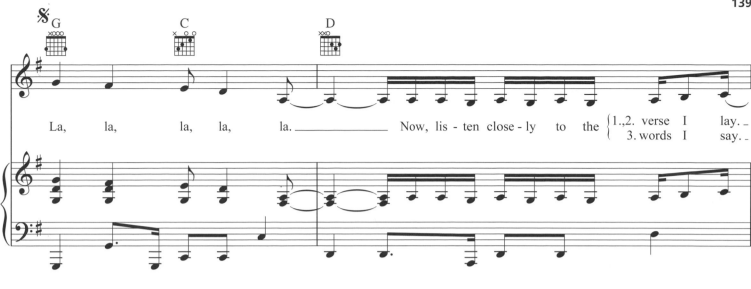

La, la, la, la, la. _____ Now, lis-ten close-ly to the {1.,2. verse I lay._
3. words I say._

____} La, ___ la, la, la, la. _____ {1.,2. It's all a-bout the word-play._
3. I'm stick-ing to the word-play._

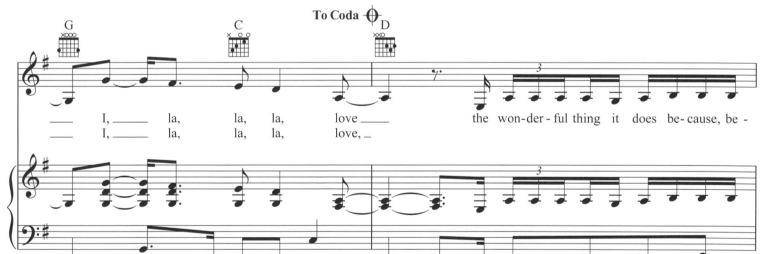

To Coda

___ I, ___ la, la, la, love ___ the won-der-ful thing it does be-cause, be-
___ I, ___ la, la, la, love, _

cause I am the wiz-ard of oohs and ahs and fa la la's, yeah, the

Mis - ter A to Z. They say I'm all a - bout the word - play.

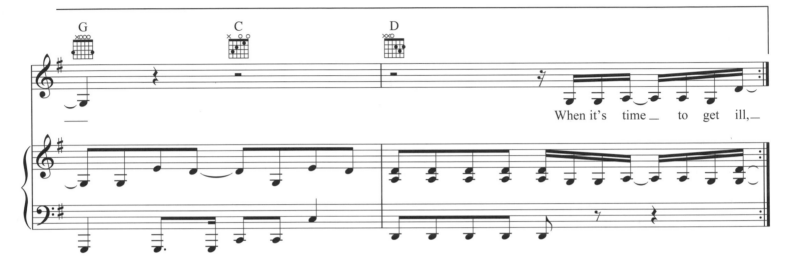

When it's time to get ill,

Mis - ter A to Z. They say I'm all a - bout the word - play. I built a

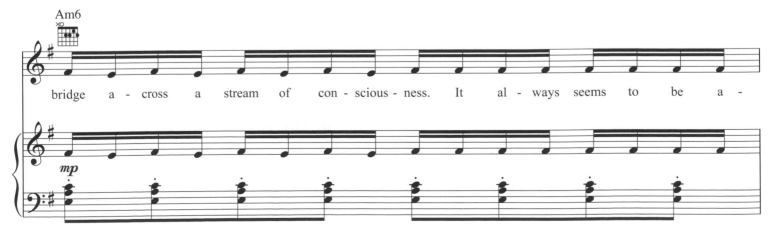

bridge a - cross a stream of con - scious - ness. It al - ways seems to be a -

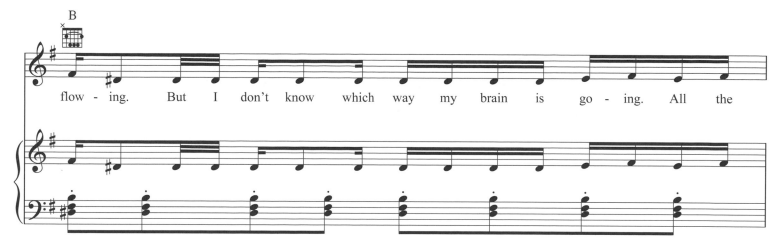

flow - ing. But I don't know which way my brain is go - ing. All the

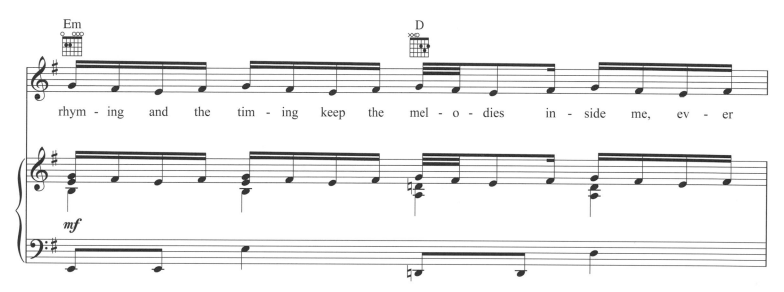

rhym - ing and the tim - ing keep the mel - o - dies in - side me, ev - er

climb - ing till I'm run - ning out of air. Are you pre -

pared to take a dive in - to the deep end of my head?

D.S. al Coda

Are you lis - ten - ing to a sin - gle word I've said?

CODA

I love the won - der - ful thing it does be - cause, be -

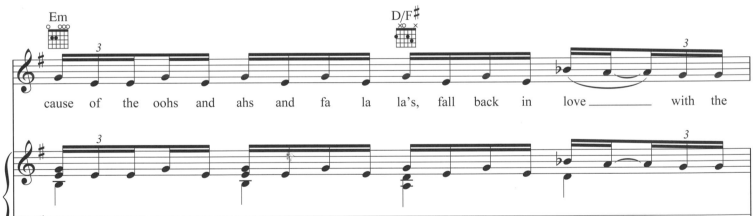

cause of the oohs and ahs and fa la la's, fall back in love _____ with the

Mis - ter A to Z, they say, is all a - bout the word - play. _____

YOU AND I BOTH

Words and Music by
JASON MRAZ

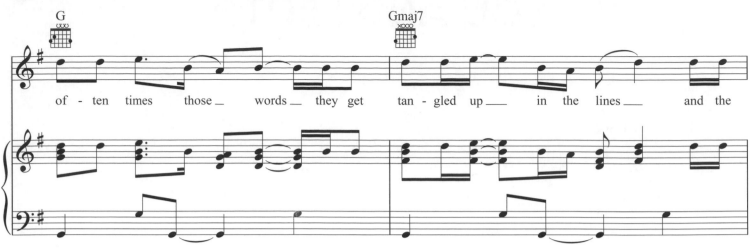

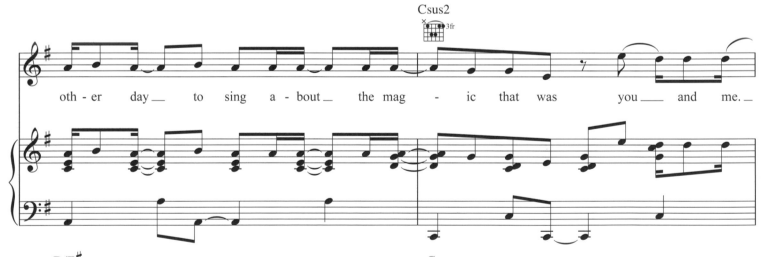

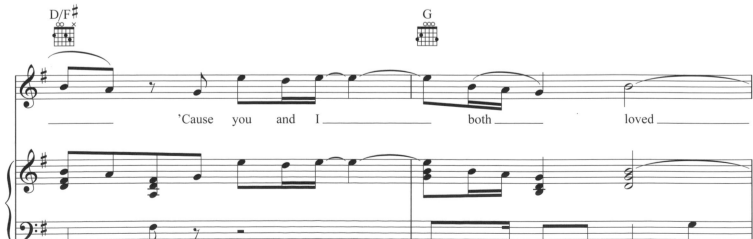

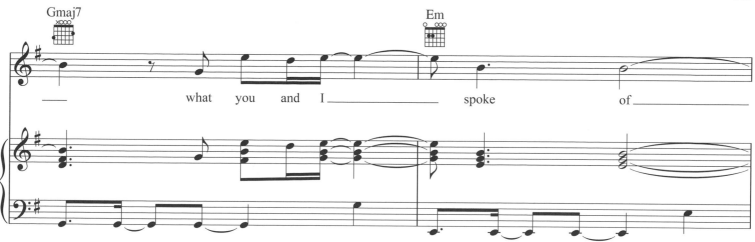

what you and I _____ spoke of _____

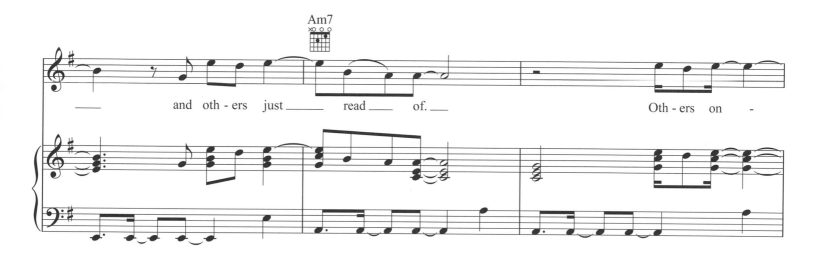

and oth-ers just _____ read _____ of. _____ Oth-ers on -

-ly read of _____ the love, _____ of the love that I _____

_____ love. _____ Yeah, _____ la, la, la, la. _____

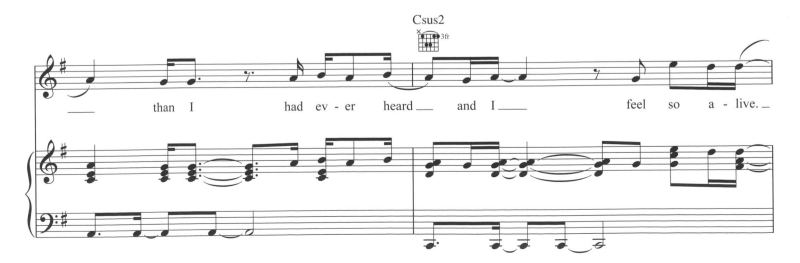

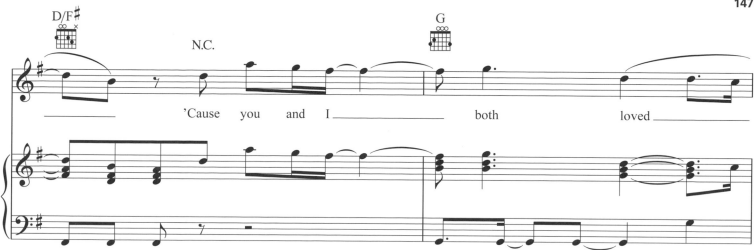

'Cause you and I _____ both _____ loved _____

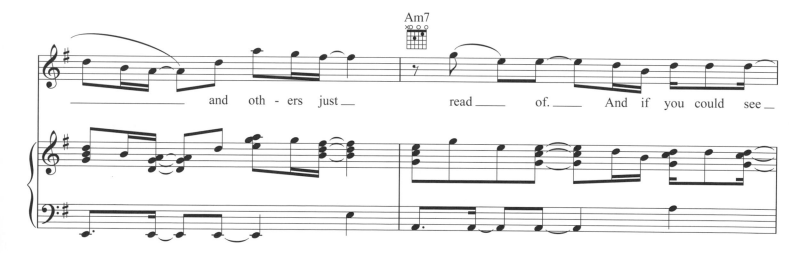

what you and I _____ spoke _____ of _____

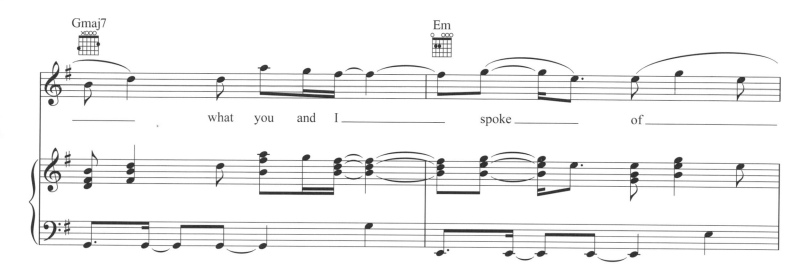

_____ and oth - ers just _____ read _____ of. _____ And if you could see _____

_____ me now. _____ Oh _____ love, _____ love _____ you and I. You and I _____

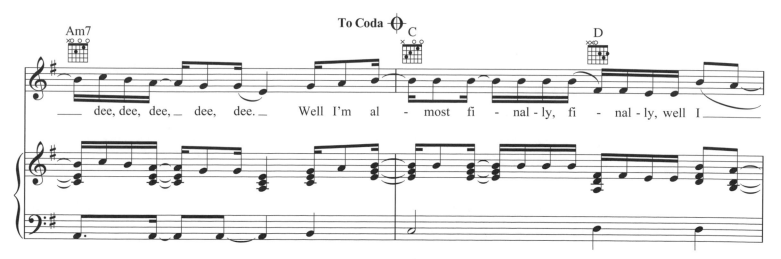

am free. Oh, _____ I'm free. And it's ___ o - kay ___

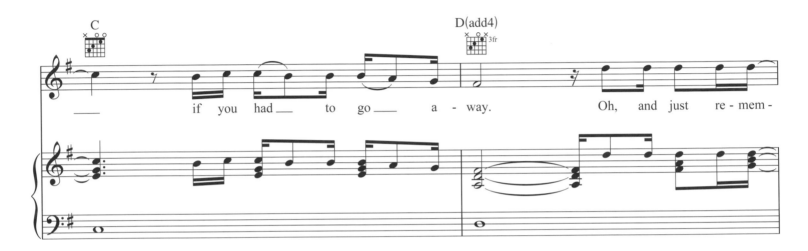

___ if you had ___ to go ___ a - way. Oh, and just re - mem -

- ber the tel - e - phones ___ will be work - in in both ___ ways. But if ___ I

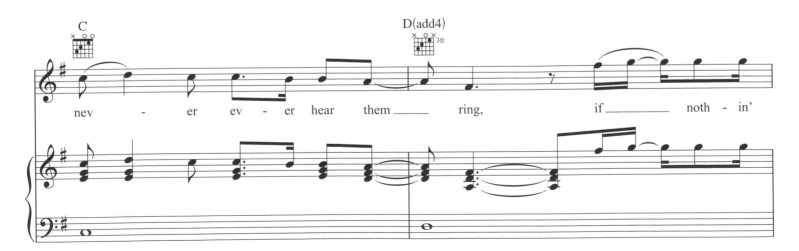

nev - er ev - er hear them _____ ring, if _____ noth - in'

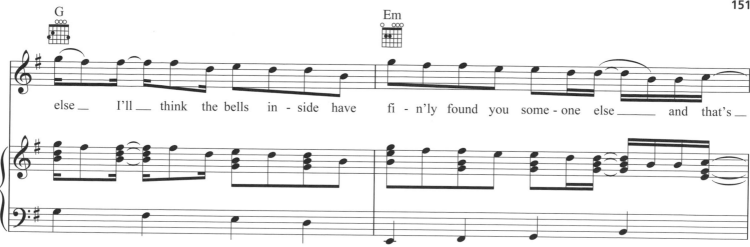

else __ I'll __ think the bells in - side have fi - n'ly found you some - one else _____ and that's __

__ o - kay _____ 'cause I'll __ re -

mem - ber ev - 'ry - thing you __ sang. ___ 'Cause you and I _____

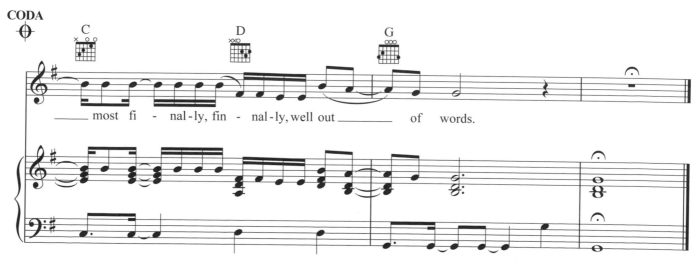

___ most fi - nal - ly, fin - nal - ly, well out ___ of words.